Antony

makes it easy

Antony
makes it easy

Antony Worrall Thompson

Antony Makes it Easy
Antony Worrall Thompson

First published in Great Britain in 2010
by Mitchell Beazley
An imprint of Octopus Publishing Group Ltd,
2–4 Heron Quays, Docklands, London E14 4JP
www.octopusbooks.co.uk

An Hachette UK company
www.hachette.co.uk

ISBN 978 1 84533 4970
A CIP record for this book is available
from the British Library

Commissioning Editor Rebecca Spry
Designer Yasia Williams-Leedham
Photographer Elizabeth Zeschin
Prop Stylist Isabel De Cordova
Home Economist Sara Lewis
Project Editor Georgina Atsiaris
Copy Editor Diona Murray-Evans
Proofreader Jo Richardson
Production Lucy Carter
Index John Noble

Set in Page Serif

Printed and bound in China
by Midas Printing International Ltd

Introduction 8

Chapter 1: Breakfast 12

Chapter 2: Lunch 46

Chapter 3: Dinner 102

Chapter 4: Vegetables 160

Chapter 5: Pudding 186

Useful Hot Sauces 216

Cold Sauces and Dips 218

Salad Dressings 219

Store Cupboard 220

Index 222

Introduction

Easy food does not always mean fast food. It's very easy to put a stew together or bung a roast in the oven, but the cooking does take time. Some recipes in this book may seem to have a lot of ingredients – you'll find this is the case when I've used Asian or Indian spices – but as I will suggest when I deal with your store cupboard, it's important to be well stocked in the spice department. They're generally not expensive and they'll last a good year.

Some of you may think the food is quite sophisticated and grown up, and you may be right, but I've included very few recipes that I wouldn't serve to my children. The earlier you start to feed your children small portions of adult food, the less fussy they'll become. Children will mimic the actions of their parents, so if you sit and eat with them a few times a week, they'll learn to trust the food.

Children like routine; they get set in their ways and have fixed views of what they do and don't like. In many cases they won't have even tried the food, but because it's different or not part of their normal food routine, they'll automatically put up the shutters. Start them off as you mean to go on and don't take no for an answer. In the end it will pay dividends.

And it's no easier for me because I'm a chef. I don't know how often I've had to say "eat your tomatoes", or "eat your mushrooms; I'm not trying to poison you, they're good for you" etc., but eventually you get there. Now I rarely get a peep out of them; everything is eaten. Not that I would call them voluntarily adventurous, but they're getting better. Well, that's the family lecture over.

The recipes here are what I would call real food, food that for the most part doesn't come out of any packets in ready-assembled, part-cooked ingredients. It's food that you cook from scratch. You'll not find food with airs or graces – no towers, little or no garnishing and certainly no foam. It's food I would serve my family and friends; kitchen table food that's good enough for the dining table too.

Real food does take longer than just bunging something in the microwave, but it needn't take much more effort or time with a little bit of planning and some preparation in advance. I'm certainly not averse to what the supermarkets have to offer for convenience. I'm not going to make my own pasta, I'm not sure I even have time to roast my own peppers and, unless I'm doing a dinner party, I'm not going to be preparing artichokes. There's nothing wrong with quality pre-prepared foods to help us along the way. Give me tinned tomatoes for 10 months of the year any day over the pale photocopies of the real thing; give me white or flageolet beans from a can; I haven't got the forethought or for that matter the time to be soaking or cooking dried beans. I've grabbed the odd tub of hummus or taramasalata in my time; nothing to be embarrassed about. I don't very often make my own stock and I don't do pastry, there's really nothing wrong with ready-roll. So these ingredients all help to make real food faster food; all I ask is that you make the effort to try and use as much fresh produce as possible.

And if I may just add one more thing, please try and get back to the seasons. We're all trying to do our bit for the planet, so let's avoid food imported from thousands of miles away. All those food miles are definitely not a good carbon footprint. Plus, I believe local seasonal food tastes so much better and still has some nutritional value. And on the subject of fresh food, please let's get out of the habit of the weekly shop. It's fine for your store cupboard ingredients – in fact, I'd rather you did a run once a month for all your cans, cleaning products, loo rolls etc., as it saves on petrol – but it's a well-known fact that the average family in the UK wastes in excess of £700 a year chucking away fresh produce that has started to rot. Buy when you need it and not in anticipation of needing it.

I'm sure you'll get food mileage out of *Antony Makes it Easy*. I want to see it well thumbed in your kitchen with the odd oil splash or tomato stain – that's what a good, well-used cookbook should be all about. Enjoy the experience and for any queries you can go to my website, **www.awtonline.co.uk.** Enjoy yourself and have lots of fun cooking and eating.

A LITTLE 'USELESS' INFORMATION ABOUT THE RECIPES.

I say 'useless' because if I said useful you'd never read them and I really want you to understand where I'm coming from. I have made an assumption that you have a useful store cupboard (see p.220), so where I say:

Store Cupboard: these are items I expect you to have. If you don't, then get stocking.

Shopping List: these are mainly fresh goods or perhaps more unusual products that you will need to buy.

Meanwhile: if you see the word 'meanwhile', it means there is no time to be sitting on your backside – while one thing is cooking, you need to be doing another task.

Alcohol: there may be the odd recipe that uses a drop. If it's a 'no cook' recipe, please omit it if the children are eating it. If it's a 'cook' recipe, then most of the alcohol will have burnt off, so it's your judgement call whether you want to use it or not....

Oven Temperatures: I have given suggested temperatures but, as you know, they vary from oven to oven, so get to know your own oven.

Recipes: always read the recipe in its entirety before commencing; that way you won't discover any hidden nasties. Always do the prep from the ingredients list first, i.e. '1 onion, finely chopped' means get chopping before starting to cook.

Eating Times: I have made suggestions for when you can eat the recipes, e.g. breakfast, dinner, but then I am a control freak, so please feel free to ignore me... if you want Soft-boiled eggs with anchovy soldiers for supper, go for it.

Quantities: all recipes are based on 4 healthy appetites. Apart from spices, most recipes will multiply up or divide down quite well.

Breakfast

Boiled

1. Take room temperature large eggs and, using a tablespoon, lower the eggs, one by one, into a small saucepan of boiling water.

2. When the water returns to the boil, reduce to a medium heat and set the timer for 4½ minutes for soft-boiled or 7 minutes for hard-boiled. Remove the eggs from the water and pop into egg cups.

3. Immediately cut the top off each egg; if you don't, the egg will continue to cook.

Poached

1. Place a saucepan filled with at least 10cm/4in cold water over a high heat. Add 1 tsp white wine vinegar for each litre/1¾pt water, then bring to the boil.

2. Break each room-temperature large egg separately into a small cup for best results, then slide the egg into the roll of the boil, reduce the heat and simmer.

3. Cook for 2–2½ minutes for a soft yolk. Lift out with a slotted spoon and drain on kitchen paper.

Antony's tip: use fresh eggs. The white straggles and odd shapes are caused from the watery whites of old eggs. The white in a fresh egg is very thick and viscous; it encloses the yolk totally and so produces the perfect poached orb.

Fried

1. Place a frying pan, preferably non-stick, over a medium heat. Add 25g/1oz unsalted butter to the pan and wait until it starts to foam but not burn brown.

2. Crack each egg separately into a small cup. Slide it into the pan and allow to set for 1 minute over a low to medium heat, then baste the yolk with the melted butter until the surface becomes opaque and the white is set. Lift out with a fish slice.

Antony's tip: many Brits cook their fried eggs in oil that's far too hot, resulting in a leathery, crispy white. My way – that is, the French way – is far more luxurious.

Scrambled

1. For each person, break 2 large eggs into a bowl, season with a pinch each of salt and ground white pepper and whisk with a fork just to bring the yolk and white together. Don't overbeat.

2. Add 25g/1oz unsalted butter to a non-stick saucepan or frying pan over a medium heat. When the butter is foaming, pour in the eggs and, with a wooden spoon, continually draw the eggs into the centre, creating curds.

3. When the eggs are nearly set to your liking, fold in 2 tbsp double cream, if you want. Immediately tip the scrambled eggs onto a plate, because if you don't, even with the heat switched off, the eggs will continue to cook.

10 minutes
prep

30 minutes
cook

A great weekend breakfast–brunch dish, full of Mediterranean flavours, that's easy to prepare in advance.

Baked eggs with chorizo and red peppers

Store Cupboard

2 garlic cloves, peeled and thinly sliced

1 small onion, diced

pinch of chilli flakes

1 tbsp olive oil

ground black pepper

4 large eggs

Shopping List

85g/3oz chorizo sausage, diced

2 smoked streaky bacon rashers, rinds removed and diced

1 small red pepper, seeded and diced

1 tomato, diced

crusty bread, for serving

1. Preheat the oven to 200°C/400°F/Gas 6. In a bowl, combine **all the ingredients except the eggs.** Season with **black pepper**, tip into a roasting tray and cook in the oven for 20 minutes.

2. Spoon the roasted mixture into 4 shallow dishes or ramekins set on a baking tray. Make a small well in the centre of each dish and break in an **egg.**

3. Place the dishes in the oven and bake for 10–12 minutes or until the egg whites have set. Sprinkle with **pepper** and serve immediately with **crusty bread.**

Antony's tip: for a less "roasted" egg, place the dishes or ramekins in a roasting tray of hot water (bain-marie) before placing in the oven.

More ideas: add half a tin of rinsed and drained chickpeas for a more substantial dish; a few drops of chilli oil dotted over the surface of the egg gives the flavour an extra kick.

Every household needs a little treat from time to time and it doesn't have to cost a fortune. For this dish try smoked salmon trimmings, which you can pick up for a song.

Posh eggs

1. Beat the **eggs** in a bowl with a fork until just combined. Don't overbeat – you only need to mix the yolks and whites together. Fold in the **horseradish sauce** and season with **salt and ground pepper**. Set aside until ready to cook.

2. Cut the **muffins** in half horizontally. Place under a hot grill, cut-side up, and cook until golden. Spread with **butter** (optional) and keep warm.

3. Place a non-stick frying pan or saucepan over a medium heat, add 45g/1½oz **butter** and cook until bubbling but not too hot. Pour in the **eggs** and stir with a wooden spoon, continually drawing the edges into the centre, until the eggs are set to your liking. Fold in the **smoked salmon.**

4. Place 2 muffin halves on each of 4 warm plates. Spoon the eggs onto the muffins and garnish with a few snipped **chives** and a sprinkling of **pepper**. Serve immediately.

Antony's tip: make sure your muffins are ready for the eggs, as the eggs will continue to cook after you've turned off the heat.

More ideas: fold in 1 tsp snipped chives or dill with the smoked salmon; substitute 4 crisp streaky bacon rashers for the smoked salmon; top with a dollop of soured cream.

Store Cupboard
8 large eggs
2 tsp horseradish sauce
salt and ground pepper
unsalted butter

Shopping List
4 English muffins
115g/4oz smoked salmon, cut into small dice
snipped chives, for garnishing

15 minutes
prep

15 minutes
cook

This has a lovely balance of flavours and makes an excellent brunch dish or starter.

Poached eggs with nice bits

Store Cupboard

unsalted butter
salt and ground black pepper
1 garlic clove, peeled and finely chopped
2 tbsp white wine vinegar
4 medium eggs

Shopping List

4 streaky bacon rashers, rinds removed and cut into strips or diced
100g/3½oz button mushrooms, sliced
100g/3½oz baby spinach, washed
4 slices bread (seeded brown is good)

1. Heat a saucepan with at least 10cm/4in boiling water.

2. Meanwhile, heat a frying pan over a medium-high heat and add 45g/1½oz **butter**. When the butter is foaming, add the **bacon** and cook until crispy (about 4 minutes). Then add the **mushrooms** and cook for 3 minutes, stirring regularly. Season with **salt and ground black pepper**. Remove the mixture from the pan and set aside to keep warm.

3. Return the pan to the heat. Add the **garlic** and cook for 2 minutes, before adding the **spinach**. You may need to do this in stages as the spinach wilts. With a pair of tongs, keep turning the spinach over. Season as it wilts. Remove from the heat and keep warm.

4. Toast the **bread** until golden, then butter each slice.

5. While making the toast, add the **vinegar** to the pan of boiling water, then crack the **eggs**, one at a time, into the roll of the boil. Reduce the heat slightly and cook the eggs for 2½ minutes. Lift out with a slotted spoon. Drain the poached eggs on kitchen paper.

6. Spoon the spinach onto the slices of buttered toast, divide the bacon and mushrooms between them and top each with a poached egg. Serve immediately.

Antony's tip: always use fresh eggs – see tip on p.15

More ideas: fry any leftover mashed potatoes until golden and crispy before folding in the mushrooms and bacon; stir 100g/3½oz cooked, flaked salmon into the bacon and mushroom mixture before serving.

This recipe is probably one for the weekend as it takes a little simple prep, but you do get the whole kit and caboodle in one dish. Leave out any ingredient that doesn't grab your fancy.

Breakfast omelette

Store Cupboard

1 tsp olive oil

1 onion, finely chopped

salt and ground white
  pepper

8 large eggs

unsalted butter

Shopping List

4 smoked back bacon
  rashers, rinds removed
  and cut into small strips

4 pork sausages, your
  favourite

115g/4oz button
  mushrooms, sliced

2 tomatoes, diced

1. Heat the **olive oil** in a frying pan over a medium heat. Add the **bacon** and cook until crispy (about 4 minutes), then remove and set aside.

2. Meanwhile, cut the **sausages** into 2.5cm/1in pieces. Add to the bacon pan, stirring from time to time and when browned but not completely cooked, add the **onion** and cook for 3 minutes until slightly softened. Add the **cooked bacon**, **mushrooms** and **tomatoes** and cook for a further 3 minutes, stirring occasionally. Season with **salt and ground white pepper**. Keep warm.

3. To prepare the omelette, beat the **eggs** and **salt and ground white pepper** in a bowl until the egg whites and yolks just come together, but don't overbeat.

4. Heat a large frying pan, add 15g/½oz **butter** and cook until foaming, then add a ladleful or a quarter of the beaten eggs. Keep the eggs moving by bringing the sides into the centre with a wooden spoon. This helps to keep the omelette fluffy. When cooked to your liking (I like it soft), add a quarter of the sausage mixture, then roll or fold your omelette.

5. Serve immediately – it's not a dish that can sit around while you cook the rest of the omelettes. Make sure you add more butter to the pan before you cook the next omelette.

More ideas: the world is your oyster, use whatever appeals – add herbs to the egg mix; scatter grated cheese over the almost-cooked omelette; use up last night's leftovers such as curries, vegetables etc.; remember that many other fillings will need precooking.

It's still my favourite breakfast – soft-boiled eggs and soldiers – but, like every chef, I've played around with different combos. Marmite soldiers, smoked salmon butter, dill butter, but my favourite is anchovy soldiers … of course, you've got to love anchovies too!

Soft-boiled eggs with anchovy soldiers

1. Place on a chopping board the **rosemary, thyme, anchovies** and **garlic** and chop until you have a fine paste. Put this in a bowl with the **butter**. Mash together with a fork.

2. Meanwhile, fill a deep saucepan with cold water and bring to the boil. Lower the **eggs**, one by one, into the boiling water and set the timer for 4½ minutes for soft yolks.

3. While the eggs are boiling, toast the **bread**, then spread the toast with the anchovy butter. Remove the crusts and cut into fingers. Chop the top off your eggs and get dipping.

Antony's tip: have your eggs at room temperature before placing them in the boiling water to stop them cracking, which will happen if they're fridge cold.

More ideas: anchovy butter is great with grilled meat or fish, so make it in larger quantities and then shape it into a sausage, wrap in cling film and keep it in the freezer, cutting off slices as required.

Store Cupboard

3 anchovy fillets in oil

½ garlic clove, peeled

55g/2oz unsalted butter, softened

8 large eggs

4–8 slices white bread

Shopping List

½ tsp finely chopped rosemary

½ tsp chopped thyme

QUICK
& EASY

10 minutes
prep

15 minutes
cook

I say naked because I've left out the pastry. This recipe makes a tasty dish that can be eaten hot, cold or at room temperature.

Naked mini breakfast quiches

Store Cupboard

unsalted butter
8 large eggs
salt and ground black
 pepper

Shopping List

12 smoked streaky bacon
 rashers, rinds removed
150ml/¼pt soured cream
8 tsp tomato relish
4 cherry tomatoes, halved

1. Preheat the oven to 180°C/350°F/Gas 4. Grease a 12-bun muffin tin or 8 ramekins with **butter.** Wrap **8 bacon rashers** around the inside of 8 of the muffin 'cups' or the ramekins. You will be left with **4 bacon rashers** to cut in half. Place 1 of the halves in the bottom of each 'cup' or ramekin.

2. In a bowl, whisk together the **eggs** and **soured cream** until you have a smooth custard. Season with **salt and ground black pepper**.

3. Place **1 tsp tomato relish** in the bottom of each 'cup', then fill with the egg custard. Top each with half a **cherry tomato** and season again. If using ramekins, place them on a baking tray.

4. Cook in the oven for 15 minutes or until set. Leave to cool slightly, then run a knife around the edge to loosen. Eat immediately, or on the run to work – there are no pastry crumbs to drop down your front!

More ideas : feel free to use double cream instead of soured cream; sprinkle the tops with herby breadcrumbs or grated cheese; replace the tomato relish with your favourite chutney or relish.

If you want to make your own pancakes, feel free, but this is an easy cookbook, so I'm allowing you to cheat. This is a breakfast-meets-snack-meets-lunch sort of dish that's good value and really quick.

Cheesy pancakes

Store Cupboard

pinch of grated nutmeg

4 sun-dried tomatoes, diced

2 tsp green or red pesto

salt and ground black pepper

extra-virgin olive oil

Shopping List

150g/5½oz ball cow's mozzarella, diced

175g/6oz ricotta or cream cheese

25g/1oz Parmesan, freshly grated

4–8 savoury pancakes or crêpes, shop bought

2 beefsteak tomatoes, each sliced into 4

1. Preheat the oven to 180°C/350°F/Gas 4. In a bowl mix the **mozzarella, ricotta or cream cheese, Parmesan, nutmeg, sun-dried tomatoes** and **pesto** until well combined. Season with a little **salt** and a generous amount of **black pepper.**

2. Lay the **pancakes or crêpes** (use 4 if you only want 1 each) on your work surface and spread the mixture over the surface of each pancake. Fold the pancakes in half, and then in half again.

3. Place them in an oiled baking dish in a single layer and top each pancake with a slice of **tomato** (or 2 slices if using only 4 pancakes). Season each slice, then drizzle with a little **olive oil**. At this stage you can cover them with cling film and refrigerate until ready to cook.

4. You can either cook in the microwave in a non-metallic baking dish by piercing the cling film and cooking on full power for 2 minutes, or remove the cling film and cook in the oven for 10–12 minutes. Serve immediately.

More ideas: add 25g/1oz toasted pine nuts to the cheese mixture; replace the mozzarella with Gorgonzola; garnish with a few basil leaves.

5 minutes
prep

10 minutes
cook

QUICK
& EASY

You can make this in advance and keep a pot in the fridge for a couple of weeks for use at short notice.

A cheese spread

1. Place the **mascarpone, cream, Gruyère** and **Gorgonzola** in a non-stick saucepan over a low heat. Stir regularly until everything has melted and mixed together. Season with a few grindings of **black pepper.** Leave to cool, then fold in the **egg yolks.** Spoon the mixture into a bowl, cover and refrigerate until ready to use.

Antony's tip: spread on toast and pop under a hot grill until bubbling and golden; cut a croissant in half horizontally, top with some cheese spread, a slice of ham and a few cooked mushrooms, then heat in the oven at 180°C/350°F/Gas 4 for about 10 minutes; hollow out a tomato, fill with cheese spread and bake in the oven for 15 minutes; stuff a large field mushroom with cheese spread, sprinkle with breadcrumbs and bake for 15 minutes; use as an omelette filling.

More ideas: try adding 55g/2oz diced crispy bacon; your favourite herb, finely chopped; some grated Parmesan for a stronger flavour.

Store Cupboard
ground black pepper
3 large egg yolks

Shopping List
200g/7oz mascarpone
150ml/¼pt double cream
150g/5½oz Gruyère, grated
150g/5½oz Gorgonzola, diced

5 minutes
prep

10 minutes
cook

Breakfast needn't just be about cereal, toast or a muffin. It can be an entertaining meal, especially if you've got someone staying over. (This isn't difficult, doesn't take long and doesn't have to be expensive.)

Breakfast bread

Store Cupboard

2 large eggs
300ml/½pt milk
25g/1oz caster sugar
55g/2oz unsalted butter
4 slices white bread
4 tsp golden syrup

Shopping List

8 unsmoked dry-cured
  streaky bacon rashers,
  rinds removed
55g/2oz toasted flaked
  almonds

1. In a flat dish, beat together the **eggs, milk** and **sugar.**

2. Gently heat 25g/1oz **butter** in a large frying pan, then dip the **bread slices,** one at a time, in the egg mix. Place 2 slices at a time in the hot butter and cook until golden brown, turn over and cook the other side. Keep warm in a low oven while cooking the remaining bread, adding more butter to the pan when required.

3. Meanwhile, under a hot grill, cook the **bacon** for about 5 minutes until golden on both sides.

4. Cut each slice of bread in half. Place 2 halves of each on 4 warm plates, top with 2 rashers of bacon, drizzle each plate with 1 tsp **golden syrup** and sprinkle with a few **toasted almonds.** Serve immediately.

More ideas: replace the golden syrup and almonds with a drizzle of fruit purée; maple syrup; a few raspberries, strawberries or blackberries tossed in caster sugar; 4 tbsp caster sugar mixed with 1 level tsp ground cinnamon.

Grabbing a sausage is one of those very satisfying moreish occasions, so I often have a plate of cold cooked sausages in the fridge. This recipe adds a different dimension to a hot dog and is far better than the normal steamed offering.

A morning hot dog

Store Cupboard
3 tbsp mango chutney

ground black pepper

olive oil, for greasing

1 tbsp wholegrain mustard

2 tbsp thick runny honey

Shopping List
8 pork sausages, your favourite

8 slices pancetta

8 hot-dog rolls

1. Preheat your oven to 200°C/400°F/Gas 6. Take each **sausage** and make a slash the length of the sausage – but not all the way through. Spoon a little **mango chutney** along the length of each sausage, then wrap each one with a slice of **pancetta.** Season with **ground black pepper**, then place the sausages on a lightly oiled baking tray and pop into the oven for 10 minutes, turning from time to time to ensure an even colouring.

2. While the sausages are cooking, mix together the **mustard** and **honey.** Paint this mixture over the sausages. Return them to the oven for 5 minutes to develop a sticky glaze.

3. Cut the **hot-dog rolls** halfway through along their length, then pop in the sausages and say thank you!

More ideas: instead of pancetta try smoked dry-cured streaky bacon; any chutney or relish, especially tomato, could replace the mango.

5 minutes
prep

5 minutes
cook

QUICK
& EASY

This is a classic Catalan speciality. It's often eaten at breakfast – as I do when visiting the local market near our house in Spain – and is a healthy way to start the day.

Chargrilled tomato bread

1. Preheat a ridged griddle pan over a high heat. Drizzle a little **olive oil** over both sides of each slice of **rustic bread**, then place the bread on the griddle pan and cook for about 1 minute each side until golden and crispy.

2. Transfer the bread to 4 plates, then sprinkle one side with a pinch of **sea salt** and rub with the **garlic clove.** Squeeze the **tomato halves** over each piece of bread, then rub the cut sides of the tomato on the bread until all you're left with is the skins. Drizzle with **olive oil.** Grind over a little **black pepper** and serve the bread at room temperature.

More ideas: why spoil such a simple, perfect thing? The only extra ingredient I'll allow you is a few shreds of basil.

Store Cupboard
extra-virgin olive oil
Maldon sea salt
1 garlic clove, peeled
ground black pepper

Shopping List
4 thick slices rustic bread
2 ripe vine tomatoes,
 halved horizontally

I love a toasted bagel. This American classic ticks all the boxes and is quick, as long as you've already done the shopping!

Smoked salmon bagels

Store Cupboard

salt and ground black
 pepper

2 tsp salted capers, rinsed
 (optional)

¼ red onion, finely
 sliced (optional)

1 lemon, cut into 4 wedges,
 for serving

Shopping List

4 plain bagels, halved
 horizontally

125g/4½oz cream cheese

125g/4½oz good-quality
 smoked salmon

1. Preheat the grill. Toast the cut side of the **bagels**, then smear with the **cream cheese.** Season with **salt and ground black pepper**.

2. Divide the **smoked salmon** between the 4 bagel bases. If desired, scatter **capers** and **red onion slices** over the salmon.

3. Replace the bagel tops. Serve with **lemon wedges**.

More ideas: replace the capers with snipped dill or fennel; add 4 crisp streaky bacon rashers to the smoked salmon; mash half a ripe avocado into the cream cheese.

10 minutes
prep

20 minutes
cook

QUICK
& EASY

A delicious breakfast offering that adds an extra dimension to the often tasteless tomato. Use a large slicing tomato – a variety like Jack Hawkins.

Herby tomatoes with toast

1. Preheat the oven to 200°C/400°F/Gas 6. Carefully remove the seeds from the **tomatoes.** Sprinkle the tomatoes with a pinch of **salt** and place, cut-side down, on kitchen paper to draw out some of the liquid.

2. Meanwhile, place the **shallot, garlic, thyme** and **anchovy fillets** in a food processor and pulse to a purée. Add **3 slices of bread, the olive oil** and **parsley** and blitz until the mixture looks like green stuffing. Place in a bowl. Fold the **bacon** into the breadcrumb stuffing and season to taste.

3. Spoon the stuffing into the tomato cavities and place the tomatoes, stuffing-side up, on a baking tray. Cook in the oven for 15–20 minutes until bubbling and golden brown.

4. Meanwhile, toast the **remaining slices of bread** until golden. Spread with **butter** or drizzle with **olive oil.** Remove the tomatoes from the oven and place 2 halves alongside each slice of toast.

Antony's tip: instead of blitzing sliced bread, buy white breadcrumbs and add an extra dash of olive oil.

More ideas: top the tomatoes with cooked crisp bacon rashers instead of adding bacon to the stuffing; this is an excellent stuffing for large cup mushrooms too – just add some vegetable stock or water to the baking tray and cook for 15 minutes.

Store Cupboard
salt and ground black pepper
2 garlic cloves, peeled
1 tsp dried thyme
5 anchovy fillets in oil
7 slices white bread
3 tbsp olive oil
unsalted butter or olive oil, for serving

Shopping List
4 large beefsteak tomatoes, halved horizontally
1 shallot, roughly chopped
1 small bunch parsley, leaves only
3 smoked streaky bacon rashers, rinds removed and diced

A useful recipe to have up your sleeve. These griddle cakes don't take too long to make and are a great base for all sorts of toppings. And yes, they're easy …

Ricotta griddle cakes with honey

Store Cupboard

125ml/4fl oz full-fat
 milk
85g/3oz plain flour, sifted
1 tsp baking powder
3 large eggs, separated
2 tbsp caster sugar
1 tsp vanilla extract
15g/½oz unsalted butter
runny honey, for serving

Shopping List

250g/9oz ricotta
fresh berries, for serving
 (optional)

1. Place the **ricotta** in a large bowl and break up with a wooden spoon or electric hand whisk. Little by little add the **milk**, whisking continuously, then gradually whisk in the **flour** mixed with the **baking powder.** Fold in the **egg yolks, sugar** and **vanilla.**

2. In a large, very clean bowl, whisk the **egg whites** until stiff. Fold a large spoonful of egg whites into the cheese mix to loosen the mixture, then gently fold in the rest of the egg whites until well combined.

3. Melt the **butter** in a large non-stick frying pan over a medium heat. When foaming, drop tablespoons of the mixture into the pan. You can cook about 4 at a time. Cook until bubbles appear on the surface of the cakes, then flip over and cook until golden (about 3 minutes). Remove with a fish slice and keep warm while you cook the remainder.

4. To serve, drizzle with **honey** and top with seasonal **berries**, if you like.

More ideas: try the griddle cakes with cooked spinach and a poached egg; crispy bacon and maple syrup; grilled Mediterranean vegetables; spread with jam; use them as a base for dips.

At school, we were given stewed prunes for breakfast. Not that there's anything particularly wrong with prunes, but they do get boring when eaten on their own. A bowl of compote, however, topped with a dollop of yoghurt, is a good combo to start to your day.

Fruity breakfast compote

1. Tip the **apricots** and **sugar** into a saucepan and cover with cold water. Place over a medium heat and simmer for 10 minutes without the lid.

2. Cut the **Bramley apple** into 16 wedges and add, with the **rhubarb**, to the apricots. Cover with a lid and simmer for 8 minutes.

3. Meanwhile, cut the **stem ginger** into small dice and add to the stewed fruit with the **ginger syrup** and **lemon juice and zest.** Simmer until the pieces of rhubarb and apple are tender but still whole.

4. Leave the compote to cool. Serve with a dollop of **Greek yoghurt.**

Antony's tip: This will keep for up to 1 week in the fridge.

More ideas: add 8 prunes at the same time as the apricots; try different dried fruits; soft fruits, such as strawberries, raspberries, blueberries and blackberries, can be added when the mixture is cool; makes a great base for a pie or crumble.

Store Cupboard
2 tbsp caster sugar

Shopping List
115g/4oz dried apricots, diced

1 large Bramley apple, peeled and cored

4 sticks rhubarb, cut into 2.5cm/1in pieces

2 pieces stem ginger and 1 tbsp ginger syrup

juice and grated zest of 1 lemon

300ml/½pt Greek yoghurt, for serving

All children love smoothies and they're a great way of consuming at least one of your five-a-day fruit and veg. You will of course require liquidizer or blender, but they're well worth the small outlay, as they're useful for soups and sauces too.

Tropical mango

Store Cupboard
150ml/¼pt coconut milk
2 tbsp runny honey
12 ice cubes

Shopping List
2 mangoes, peeled, stoned and roughly chopped
500ml/18fl oz Greek yoghurt
2 bananas, peeled and broken up into chunks
6 mint leaves (optional)

1. Place everything in a liquidizer or blender and whiz until smooth and creamy.

2. Divide between 4 glasses.

Raspberry and banana

Store Cupboard
2 tbsp runny honey
150ml/¼pt milk
12 ice cubes

Shopping List
115g/4oz raspberries
2 bananas, peeled and broken up into chunks
2 tbsp raspberry coulis or sauce
500ml/18fl oz Greek yoghurt

1. Place everything in a liquidizer or blender and whiz until smooth and creamy.

2. Divide between 4 glasses.

Antony's tip: if you use frozen berries, then you can leave out the ice cubes.

Strawberry, lemon and mint

Store Cupboard
12 ice cubes

Shopping List
225g/8oz strawberries, hulled
juice and grated zest of 2 lemons
700ml/1¼pt lemonade
6 mint leaves

1. Place everything in a liquidizer or blender and whiz until smooth and thick.

2. Divide between 4 glasses.

Pineapple passion

Store Cupboard
12 ice cubes

Shopping List
1 small tin pineapple chunks in juice
2 passion fruit, pulp only
1 large banana, peeled and broken up into chunks
300ml/½pt pineapple juice
500ml/18fl oz Greek yoghurt

1. Place everything in a liquidizer or blender and whiz until smooth and creamy.

2. Divide between 4 glasses.

More ideas: try kiwi fruit with elderflower cordial, grapefruit juice and ice cubes; frozen tropical fruits with orange juice and chocolate ice-cream.

Lunch

A wonderful après-ski dish: potatoes with smoked bacon and melting cheese. I can see a pint of beer going down well with this.

Tartiflette

Store Cupboard

2 tbsp olive oil

2 onions, thinly sliced

2 garlic cloves, peeled and thinly sliced

675g/1½lb waxy salad potatoes, e.g. Anya, Pink Fir or Charlotte, scrubbed and sliced

unsalted butter

salt and ground black pepper

Shopping List

4 smoked back bacon rashers, rinds removed and diced

1 tsp thyme leaves, chopped

115g/4oz Gruyère, grated

chicory salad, for serving

1. Heat a large frying pan with the **olive oil.** Add the **bacon, onion** and **garlic** and cook over a medium heat for about 8 minutes until the onion has softened and the bacon is starting to crisp.

2. Add the **potatoes, thyme** and **butter**, toss to combine and season. Cover with a lid and cook for 20 minutes, turning everything over from time to time.

3. When the potatoes are tender, scatter the **Gruyère** over the potatoes, cover again and cook until the cheese melts (about 6 minutes).

4. Place the pan in the middle of the table for everyone to serve themselves. This is excellent with a chicory salad.

Antony's tip: to speed things up, cook the potatoes until tender in boiling salted water, drain, then fry.

More ideas: add 200ml/7fl oz double cream halfway through cooking (as in this photo).

The baked potato is a staple food for many throughout the land, but fillings can get a bit mundane: baked beans, grated cheese, mince ... Here's one that promises to lift the potato experience.

This year's model baked potato

Store Cupboard

4 floury potatoes, e.g. Vales Sovereign, Maris Piper or King Edward, scrubbed

2 tsp horseradish sauce

55g/2oz unsalted butter, softened

salt and ground black pepper

Shopping List

115g/4oz smoked streaky bacon rashers, rinds removed and diced

100g/3½oz cream cheese

150g/5½oz ball cow's mozzarella, diced

225g/8oz or 2 hot smoked salmon fillets

1. Preheat the oven to 200°C/400°F/Gas 6. Bake the **potatoes** on a rack over a roasting tray for 1¼–1½ hours (depending on the size of the spud) until the skins are crisp and the flesh soft and cooked through.

2. Meanwhile, in a frying pan over a medium heat, cook the **bacon** until crisp and golden (about 5 minutes), drain on kitchen paper and set aside.

3. In a bowl, mash together the **horseradish sauce**, **cream cheese** and **butter** until well blended. Season, then fold in the crisp bacon pieces and **mozzarella.** Flake the **salmon**, discarding the skin and checking for bones.

4. Remove the potatoes from the oven. When cool enough to handle, cut them in half, scoop out the flesh into a bowl and mash with a fork. Combine with the cream cheese mixture and gradually fold in the flaked salmon. Spoon the mixture back into the potato shells and return to the oven for 15–20 minutes. Serve piping hot.

More ideas: substitute diced avocado for the salmon; add a handful of cooked tiger prawns; add a few snipped chives; sweat 1 small finely diced onion in butter with the bacon.

10 minutes
prep

25 minutes
cook

SLOW
& EASY

Field mushrooms, also known by the American name Portobello, are a great "meaty" experience. They provide exceptional value when you consider a large one can replace a piece of meat or fish.

Roast field mushrooms with bacon, anchovy and tomato

1. Put the **olive oil** in a frying pan over a high heat. Add the **bacon** and fry until golden and crispy (about 5 miutes). Remove and set aside. Reduce the heat.

2. Leave the pan over the heat. Remove the stalks from the **mushrooms** and put the mushroom caps in the frying pan with 2 tbsp **water.** Cover with a lid and cook for 6 minutes. Remove the mushrooms and keep warm.

3. Add the **garlic, anchovies, tomatoes, shallot** and **chilli flakes** to the same pan and cook over a medium heat for 8 minutes, before adding the **paprika** and **spinach.** Cook until the spinach wilts. Season. Add the **soured cream**, stir to combine and check the seasoning. Bring to the boil and cook for 1 minute.

4. Place the mushrooms on 4 warm places. Spoon over the chunky sauce and scatter with the crispy bacon.

Antony's tip: adding water speeds up the mushroom cooking process.

More ideas: feel free to leave out the anchovies; chop the mushroom stalks and add them to the sauce; substitute diced roasted peppers (from a jar) for the cherry tomatoes.

Store Cupboard

1 tbsp olive oil

2 garlic cloves, peeled and finely sliced

2 anchovy fillets in oil, roughly chopped

½ tsp chilli flakes

1 tsp sweet paprika

salt and ground black pepper

Shopping List

115g/4oz lardons or bacon pieces

4 large field (Portobello) mushrooms

1 punnet cherry tomatoes, halved

1 shallot, finely diced

2 handfuls of spinach, tough stalks removed and washed

300ml/½pt soured cream

5 minutes
prep

15 minutes
cook

QUICK
& EASY

I'm not asking you to make gnocchi – mind you, it's not that difficult. However, there are some very acceptable versions in the shops. I think you'll like this bowl.

Gnocchi nuggets with creamy peas and prosciutto

1. Cut the **prosciutto** into 1cm/½in strips. Heat a frying pan with **olive oil** and fry the prosciutto for 2 minutes over a medium heat, stirring regularly, until golden. Drain on kitchen paper and allow to crisp.

2. Meanwhile, whisk the **eggs, cream, Parmesan** and **chives** over a very gentle heat; do not allow to boil.

3. Bring a saucepan of salted water to the boil, add the **peas** and boil for 5 minutes. Remove with a slotted spoon and keep the pea water to cook the gnocchi. Roughly mash the peas with a fork or potato masher, then add them to the cream mixture. Season to taste.

4. Tip the **gnocchi** into the boiling pea water and cook until they've all floated to the surface. Drain well, then add the gnocchi to the pea sauce. Warm through over a low heat for about 1 minute; do not boil or the sauce will curdle. Divide between 4 warm bowls and top with the crispy prosciutto. Serve immediately.

More ideas: if prosciutto is not on your shopping list, use smoked dry-cured streaky bacon, although it probably won't get as crispy; use Greek yoghurt instead of double cream.

Store Cupboard

1 tbsp olive oil

2 large eggs

40g/1½oz Parmesan, freshly grated

salt and ground black pepper

Shopping List

85g/3oz prosciutto (Parma or Serrano ham)

300ml/½pt double cream

2 tbsp snipped chives

225g/8oz peas, fresh or frozen

500g/1lb 2oz potato gnocchi

Chorizo is not an Italian sausage, but who cares, it's the flavour that counts. I like this combination, and I'm sure if the Italians ate it they would like it too ... Gino D'Acampo, your verdict please.

Penne with squid and chorizo

1. Heat a large saucepan of salted water until boiling. Pour in the **penne** and stir for 2 minutes to prevent it sticking. Cook for 1 minute less than the manufacturer's instructions.

2. Meanwhile, heat a large frying pan with 2 tbsp **olive oil** until almost smoking, then add the **chorizo** and fry over a high heat until crisp and releasing its fat (about 1½ minutes per side). Remove with a slotted spoon and set aside to keep warm.

3. To the same pan add the **squid** and cook for no more than 1 minute, stirring regularly. Remove and place with the chorizo. Add the **garlic** to the pan and cook over a medium heat until it starts to turn golden. Add the **chilli flakes, roasted peppers, rosemary** and **tomatoes.** Bring to the boil, cook for 5 minutes until thick and season to taste.

4. Meanwhile, drain the pasta. Return the squid and chorizo to the sauce, toss to combine, then tip in the penne. Mix well and serve drizzled with **olive oil.**

More ideas: forget the pasta and use 400g/14oz tin chickpeas (rinsed and drained) instead; a handful of spinach thrown into the sauce will add nutrients.

Store Cupboard
325g/11½oz dried penne
3 tbsp extra-virgin olive oil
2 garlic cloves, peeled and crushed
pinch of chilli flakes
400g/14oz tin chopped tomatoes
salt and ground black pepper

Shopping List
175g/6oz chorizo sausage, sliced
225g/8oz cleaned baby squid, cut into rings
3 roasted peppers (from a jar), diced
1 tsp finely chopped rosemary

10 minutes
prep

20 minutes
cook

Supermarkets provide lots of choice in stuffed pastas, but the range of sauces is not up to scratch, with hardly any new varieties appearing over the last few years. Here's an idea …

How to excite ready-made tortellini

Store Cupboard

25g/1oz unsalted butter
2 garlic cloves, peeled and crushed
50ml/2fl oz dry white wine
salt
55g/2oz Parmesan, freshly grated

Shopping List

4 smoked dry-cured back bacon rashers, rinds removed and chopped into lardons
1 leek, thinly sliced
¼ Savoy cabbage, finely shredded
225g/8oz button mushrooms, thickly sliced
1 tsp thyme leaves
300ml/½pt double cream
500g/1lb 2oz tortellini, your favourite

1. Melt the **butter** in a large frying pan, then add the **bacon** and fry over a medium heat until golden and crisp (about 4 minutes). Add the **leek, garlic** and **cabbage** and cook for 1 minute before adding the **mushrooms.**

2. Cook for 5 minutes, stirring occasionally, then add the **thyme** and **wine.** Boil until most of the liquid has evaporated (about 5 minutes). Stir in the **double cream** and simmer for 5 minutes until the sauce has thickened.

3. Meanwhile bring a large pan of salted water to the boil. Cook the **tortellini** according to the manufacturer's instructions. Drain. Fold the **Parmesan** into the cream sauce, then add the tortellini, stir to combine and serve immediately.

More ideas: add 225g/8oz cooked, flaked salmon to the sauce – it's lovely with any sort of pasta; try 115g/4oz diced chorizo sausage instead of the bacon, with some chopped roasted peppers (from a jar) instead of the cabbage.

15 minutes
prep

10 minutes
cook

QUICK
& EASY

I reckon we all desire a burger from time to time, but some of us take the lazy route via Maccy D. Here's a beefburger influenced by the East.

A burger with attitude

1. Put into a bowl the **curry paste, beef mince, half the coriander, half the mint** and **ginger.** Mix well and season. Divide the mixture into 4 and shape, not into normal round "burgers", but into oval "torpedoes" to fit into the pittas. Put the **olive oil** in a frying pan over a medium heat, then cook the 4 burgers for about 3 minutes each side or until cooked through.

2. Meanwhile, combine the **cucumber, spring onions, remaining coriander, remaining mint, garlic, tomato** and **yoghurt** in a bowl and set aside.

3. Heat the **pitta bread** for 1 minute each side in a dry frying pan over a low heat. Cut a pocket in each pitta down one side, stuff in some **rocket**, followed by a burger, then turn the pitta on its side and drizzle in the savoury yoghurt. Then go for it: these burgers beat those found on the high street any day.

More ideas: instead of the yoghurt, drizzle in some sweet chilli sauce; leave out the yoghurt, but mix the salad with the juice of half a lime.

Store Cupboard

1 tbsp Thai red curry paste

2.5cm/1in root ginger, peeled and grated

salt and ground black pepper

1 tbsp olive oil

1 garlic clove, peeled and crushed

Shopping List

450g/1lb best beef mince

3 tbsp finely chopped coriander

4 tsp finely chopped mint

¼ cucumber, cut into small dice

3 spring onions, finely diced

1 tomato, seeded and diced

100g/3½oz Greek yoghurt

4 pitta bread

handful of rocket leaves

There's a time and a place for a sandwich, but this is the time and place for a wrap … no crumbs, no dropped filling, (unless you forget to tuck in the ends), and innumerable tasty combos.

Tortilla wrap with Moroccan lamb

1. In a large frying pan over a high heat, fry the **lamb mince** in the **olive oil** for 5–6 minutes to brown and cook through, remove with a slotted spoon and drain on kitchen paper.

2. Drain off some of the lamb fat and turn down the heat under the pan. Add the **chopped onion, garlic, all the spices** and a pinch of **salt** and cook gently for 6 minutes. Stir in the browned lamb and cook for 1 minute. Season.

3. Lay out the **tortillas** and spread with the mince mixture, leaving a 2.5cm/1in border all the way round. Scatter over the **red onion slices, tomato** and **chopped coriander** and drizzle with **yoghurt**. Roll up the tortilla, tucking in the ends. Slice in half through the centre, then enjoy.

More ideas: use flatbread instead of tortillas; spread the tortilla with hummus before scattering with lamb; add a handful of toasted pine nuts; substitute chicken mince for the lamb, but fry for longer until the chicken is completely cooked.

Store Cupboard
2 tbsp olive oil
1 onion, finely chopped
2 garlic cloves, peeled and finely chopped
½ tsp ground cinnamon
½ tsp ground cumin
½ tsp ground coriander
½ tsp ground turmeric
¼ tsp chilli powder
½ red onion, thinly sliced
salt and ground black pepper

Shopping List
325g/11½oz lamb mince
4 soft flour tortillas
2 tomatoes, diced
½ bunch coriander, roughly chopped
4 tbsp Greek yoghurt

Meatballs appeal to all ages. The key is to use lamb or chicken, which cook in a short time, but what else you put in them is up to you.

Speedy meatballs with tomato and penne

Store Cupboard

2 tbsp olive oil

1 onion, roughly chopped

2 garlic cloves, peeled and crushed

1 tsp dried oregano

pinch of chilli flakes

2 x 400g/14oz tins chopped tomatoes

150ml/¼pt dry white wine

1 tsp caster sugar

25g/1oz Parmesan, freshly grated, plus extra for serving

1 large egg, beaten

3 tbsp soft white breadcrumbs

salt and ground black pepper

350g/12oz dried penne

Shopping List

450g/1lb lamb mince

2 tbsp finely chopped oregano or marjoram

2 tbsp red pepper pesto

1. Place a large saucepan over a medium heat, add the **olive oil, onion, garlic, dried oregano** and **chilli flakes** and cook gently for 10 minutes before adding the **tomatoes, wine** and **sugar.** Simmer for 10 minutes until the sauce starts to thicken.

2. Meanwhile, in a large bowl combine the **lamb mince, fresh oregano or marjoram, pesto, Parmesan, egg** and **breadcrumbs.** Season, then squidge the mixture together with your hands. Roll into 16 small balls.

3. Add the meatballs to the tomato sauce and simmer for 15 minutes until they're cooked through. Check the sauce for seasoning.

4. At the same time, put a large pan of salted water on to boil. When it's boiling, tip in the **penne** and stir for 2 minutes to prevent it sticking. Cook for 1 minute less than the manufacturer's instructions.

5. Drain and add the dripping pasta to the meatball sauce. Toss to combine and serve with grated Parmesan.

More ideas: for a richer sauce, add 1 tbsp sun-dried tomato paste; substitute fresh basil for the fresh oregano or marjoram; add 55g/2oz chopped pancetta to the onion when making the sauce.

Asian broths are always exciting, fresh, vibrant and really easy as long as you've already got the ingredients.

The ultimate pot noodle

Store Cupboard

4 lime leaves, crumbled

2.5cm/1in root ginger, peeled and grated

2 garlic cloves, peeled and roughly chopped

2 tsp palm sugar or soft dark brown sugar

2 tsp Thai fish sauce (nam pla)

115g/4oz instant (ready-cooked) egg noodles

salt and ground black pepper

Shopping List

2 x 415g/14½oz tins chicken or beef consommé

1 hot red chilli, sliced

½ bunch coriander, leaves and stalks, roughly chopped

1 bonelss, skinless chicken breast, thinly sliced into strips

6 shiitake mushrooms, thinly sliced

8 raw tiger prawns, peeled

juice of 1 lime

1. Place the **consommé** in a saucepan and bring to a simmer over a medium heat.

2. Meanwhile, in a mini blender or using a mortar and pestle, blend together the **lime leaves, chilli, ginger, garlic** and **coriander** to a smooth paste. Add the paste to the stock and cook gently for 3 minutes, then add the **chicken strips** and **shiitake mushrooms.** Simmer for 3 minutes.

3. Stir in the **prawns, lime juice, palm or soft brown sugar, fish sauce** and **noodles.** Cook for about 3 minutes until the prawns turn pink and the chicken is cooked through. Check the seasoning and serve piping hot.

More ideas: any green vegetables – pak choi, broccoli florets, sugar snap peas, French beans, asparagus, mangetout – can be added with the chicken towards the end of cooking.

5 minutes prep

35 minutes cook

This 'sandwich' is so easy once you've mastered the garlic purée and the combination of flavours is hard to beat.

Prawn, bacon and garlic pitta pockets

Store Cupboard

125ml/4fl oz full-fat milk

4 garlic cloves, peeled

55g/2oz Parmesan

olive oil

salt and ground black pepper

Shopping List

150ml/¼pt double cream

8 smoked streaky bacon rashers, rinds removed

16 raw tiger prawns, peeled

4 pitta breads

handful of rocket leaves

1. Put the **milk** and **garlic** in a small saucepan and simmer for 20 minutes, topping up with extra milk as necessary. Drain and discard the milk. Return the garlic to the pan with the **cream** and **half the Parmesan**, grated. Cook for about 5 minutes until the cream has reduced by two-thirds, then tip the garlic and cream into a mini food processor and blend to a smooth purée.

2. Heat a ridged griddle pan and smear with a little **olive oil.** Cook the **bacon** over a high heat until golden and crispy, turning once. Remove and keep warm. In the same pan, cook the **tiger prawns** until pink and cooked through (about 1 minute each side). Remove and season.

3. Toast the **pittas** in the same pan for 30 seconds on each side, then cut a pocket along the side of each. Spoon the garlic purée into the pockets followed by the **rocket leaves**, 4 prawns and 2 rashers of bacon. Finish with shavings of the **remaining Parmesan**.

Antony's tip: the best way to get Parmesan shavings is simply to use a potato peeler.

More ideas: this pitta filling makes an excellent bruschetta topping; try swapping the prawns for 8 cleaned diver-caught scallops, cooked for about 1 minute each side.

10 minutes
prep

15 minutes
cook

QUICK
& EASY

I'm a bit of a fan of nasi goreng. There are so many different recipes, but I like a bowl of this one from time to time, and so do my children.

A bowl of nice rice

1. Heat an omelette pan or small frying pan over a medium heat with **1 tbsp vegetable oil.** Pour in a third of the **beaten eggs** and swirl it over the base, as you would do for a pancake, so that the omelette is very thin. Cook until set (about 1 minute), then turn out. Make 2 more omelettes using fresh **vegetable oil** every time. When they are cool enough to handle, roll up and slice thinly.

2. Put **2 tbsp vegetable oil** in a wok over a medium heat and stir-fry the **onion, ginger, garlic** and **chilli flakes** for 3–4 minutes so that the onion retains its texture and is still firm.

3. Add the **sesame oil, cooked rice, oyster sauce, soy sauce** and **sugar.** Stir-fry until the rice is hot and a little crusty (about 3 minutes), then add the **cabbage** and cook for 2 minutes. Fold in the omelette strips, **prawns, chicken, beansprouts** and **coriander.**

4. Stir-fry until the mixture is hot, season and serve immediately.

More ideas: nasi goreng is Indonesian fried rice, so it's a great way of using up all sorts of hidden fridge beauties.

Store Cupboard

5 tbsp vegetable oil

3 large eggs, beaten

2 onions, finely sliced

2.5cm/1in root ginger, peeled and grated

2 garlic cloves, peeled and thinly sliced

½ tsp chilli flakes

1 tsp sesame oil

325g/12oz freshly cooked rice

2 tbsp oyster sauce

2 tbsp dark soy sauce

2 tbsp soft dark brown sugar

salt and ground black pepper

Shopping List

¼ Savoy cabbage, finely shredded

16 chilled tiger prawns in brine, drained

225g/8oz cooked chicken, shredded

handful of beansprouts

1 small bunch coriander, finely chopped

10 minutes
prep

25 minutes
cook

You can buy a perfectly acceptable chicken sandwich, but for flavour it won't touch this spicy roll with crispy skinned chicken. Who could resist it? Not me, that's for sure.

Spiced chicken rolls

Store Cupboard

Maldon sea salt

juice and grated zest of
 ½ lemon

2 tsp Cajun seasoning

3 tbsp olive oil

1 onion, cut into 8 wedges

8 garlic cloves, peeled

2 tbsp good-quality
 mayonnaise

Shopping List

4 boneless chicken thighs,
 skin on

1 beefsteak tomato, cut
 into 4 slices

4 crusty bread rolls, halved
 horizontally

1. Preheat the oven to 190°C/375°F/Gas 5. Sprinkle the **chicken thighs** with a pinch of **salt**, **the lemon juice** and **Cajun seasoning.** Massage the mixture into the skin and flesh.

2. Lightly coat the bottom of an ovenproof frying pan with **1 tbsp olive oil.** Place the chicken, skin-side down, in the frying pan and cook over a medium heat for 5 minutes, then place another clean ovenproof frying pan or saucepan on top of the chicken to weigh it down. Place in the oven for about 18 minutes, until cooked all the way through.

3. Meanwhile, put the **remaining olive oil, onion wedges, garlic** and **tomato slices** in a small roasting tin in a single layer, pop it into the oven and cook for 18 minutes.

4. Mix the **mayonnaise** and **lemon zest** and spread on the bases of the **crusty bread rolls.** Pile the tomato mixture on top of the mayo, place the chicken, skin-side up, on top, then sandwich with the other half of the roll. Eat ...

More ideas: use an Indian or Moroccan Spice mix instead of Cajun; you may prefer the tomatoes raw, but I just love overcooked squidgy tomatoes.

10 minutes
prep

10 minutes
cook

QUICK
& EASY

A lovely simple lunch: an open sandwich that fills you up.

Warm smoked duck, cherry tomato and rocket bruschetta

1. Place a ridged griddle pan and a frying pan over a medium heat. Cut the **ciabatta** in half horizontally, then in half again vertically, giving you 4 equal-sized pieces of bread. Coat the cut surfaces of the ciabatta with **olive oil** and place, cut side down, in the griddle pan. Depending on the size of the pan, you may need to do this in 2 hits. Cook until one side is golden; do not turn over. Remove from the heat and rub the oiled surface of each slice with the **garlic.**

2. Meanwhile, put the **cherry tomatoes** in the hot frying pan with 2 tbsp **olive oil.** Fry over a high heat until the tomatoes start to split (about 5 minutes).

3. Slice the **duck breast** across its width into 16 pieces, then add to the tomatoes. Toss until warmed through. Add the **vinegar** and season. Toss to combine, add the **rocket** and very briefly toss together. Divide the mixture between the 4 pieces of ciabatta and serve immediately.

Antony's tip: you can buy ready-sliced smoked smoked duck breast in most supermarkets.

More ideas: use smoked chicken instead of duck, raw baby spinach instead of rocket and roasted peppers (from a jar) instead of tomatoes.

Store Cupboard
extra-virgin olive oil
1 garlic clove, peeled
1 tbsp balsamic vinegar
salt and ground black
 pepper

Shopping List
1 ciabatta
12 cherry tomatoes
1 smoked duck breast
handful of rocket leaves

Beetroot is one of those root vegetables that children often turn away from, which is a shame as we're now told it is one of nature's superfoods. There seems to be no reason except that not many of us use it as a vegetable. It should appeal, as it is sweet; we've just got to get around the colour.

Peppered smoked mackerel with beetroot and horseradish

1. Place half the **beetroot**, the **olive oil, honey** and **wine** in a food processor and blend until smooth. Scrape into a bowl and season.

2. Remove the skin from the **smoked mackerel** and cut each fillet in half lengthways. Combine the **soured cream** with the **horseradish sauce** and **Tabasco**.

3. Put a spoonful of beetroot purée in the centre of the plate. Slice the remaining beetroot and lay a few slices on the plate. Top with 2 mackerel fillets and garnish with **watercress or rocket** and a dollop of the horseradish mixture.

4. Serve with **brown or soda bread.**

Antony's tip: cook raw beetroot for anything from 40 minutes to 1½ hours, depending on the size. Never trim off the root or stalk ends before cooking, as the beetroot will bleed into the water. To peel, don't use a knife or peeler, just pop on a pair of rubber gloves and rub the skin off.

More ideas: I'm a massive fan of smoked eel, and it makes a great partner to beetroot.

Store Cupboard

1 tbsp extra-virgin olive oil
2 tsp runny honey
splash of red wine
salt and ground black pepper
2 tbsp horseradish sauce
few drops of Tabasco

Shopping List

250g/9oz cooked unpickled beetroot, peeled and roughly chopped
4 peppered smoked mackerel fillets
150ml/¼pt soured cream
2 handfuls of watercress or rocket leaves
brown or soda bread, for serving

I love sushi and sashimi; such beautiful textures, such freshness. I can't think of anything I'd rather eat, but I have to accept that they're not everyone's cup of tea, so here a little added marinade is the order of the day.

DIY salmon sashimi with flavour

Store Cupboard

1cm/½in root ginger,
  peeled and grated

1 garlic clove, peeled and
  crushed

2 tbsp light soy sauce

1 tsp rice vinegar

1 tsp runny honey

juice and grated zest
  of 1 lime

1 tsp sesame oil

Shopping List

1 hot red chilli, seeded
  and finely diced

325g/11½oz skinless,
  centre-cut salmon fillet

2 tsp roughly chopped
  coriander

handful of watercress
  sprigs

1. To make the marinade, stir together the **ginger, garlic, chilli, soy sauce, vinegar, honey, lime juice** and **sesame oil.**

2. Carve the **salmon** straight across the fillet into "D"-shaped slices about 5mm/¼in thick. Check for bones. Mix with the marinade, cover and leave at room temperature for 30 minutes.

3. Arrange the salmon slices in the centre of 4 plates. Drizzle with the marinade and sprinkle with the **lime zest, coriander** and **watercress.** Serve immediately.

Antony's tip: don't marinate for longer than 30 minutes, as most fish (apart from mackerel, herring and sardines) is delicately flavoured.

More ideas: try this treatment with sliced tuna, sea bass, sea bream, scallops or whole peeled fresh prawns.

How easy can food get? This pâté is perfect as a starter or a nibble, and it's perfect for unexpected guests ... just as long as you've got a food processor.

Smoked fish pâté

Store Cupboard

85g/3oz unsalted butter, softened

2 tsp horseradish sauce

½ tsp cayenne pepper

¼ tsp ground nutmeg

juice of 1 lemon

salt and ground black pepper

Shopping List

4 smoked mackerel fillets, skin removed and roughly chopped

150g/5½oz cream cheese

115g/4oz smoked salmon trimmings, diced

1 tbsp snipped chives

crusty bread, for serving

1. Place the **mackerel, cream cheese, butter, horseradish, cayenne, nutmeg** and **lemon juice** in a food processor and blend until smooth. Scrape into a bowl, then fold in the **smoked salmon** and **chives.** Season and serve with **crusty bread.**

More ideas: substitute kippers or hot smoked salmon for the smoked mackerel; for a dinner party starter, spoon the pâté into little pots, smooth flat and top with melted butter.

The majority of the public seems to love the classic avocado with prawns, but there's no reason why you shouldn't give it a little twist. Little Gem lettuce leaves make the perfect containers for this salad.

A twist on avocado with prawns

1. Stir together the **mayo, sweet chilli sauce, hot chilli sauce, soured cream** and **tomato ketchup** to make the dressing.

2. In a large bowl, combine the **avocado, spring onions** and **prawns.** Add enough dressing to coat everything generously. Arrange the **lettuce leaves** on 4 plates and spoon the salad into the centre of the leaves.

Antony's tip: prepare the avocado at the last minute to prevent it discolouring.

More ideas: use the smaller pink North Atlantic prawns instead of the tiger prawns to be more eco-friendly.

Store Cupboard

2 tbsp good-quality mayonnaise

2 tbsp sweet chilli sauce

1 tsp hot chilli sauce

1 tbsp good-quality tomato ketchup

Shopping List

2 tbsp soured cream

1 avocado, peeled, stoned and cut into small dice

2 spring onions, finely sliced

225g/8oz tiger prawns in brine, drained

2 Little Gem lettuce, leaves separated

Every home cook I know thinks squid is tricky to deal with. It's actually really simple as long as you follow the rules. Squid needs to be cooked in a flash or long and slow; there's no inbetween. This salad is a quickie.

An Asian squid salad

Store Cupboard

3 garlic cloves, peeled and
  roughly chopped

2 tbsp soft dark brown
  sugar

1cm/½in root ginger,
  peeled and roughly
  chopped

juice and grated zest of
  1 lime

2 tbsp light soy sauce

2 tbsp vegetable oil

Shopping List

1 bunch coriander, cut in
  4 down the length of the
  stalk

3 medium hot green
  chillies, roughly chopped

½ stem lemongrass,
  outer skin removed and
  roughly chopped

4 cleaned, medium-sized
  squid, in tubes

2 handfuls of frisée lettuce,
  or other salad greens

1. Place the **coriander, garlic, sugar, chillies, lemongrass** and **ginger** in a food processor and blitz until you have a smoothish purée. You'll need to scrape the sides down once or twice. Put into a bowl and mix in the **lime juice and zest** and **soy sauce.**

2. Now take the squid tubes and cut down the length of a side, opening up the squid to reveal the inside, which you may need to rinse with cold running water if there is grit or any innards present. Cut each tube in half, giving you 8 pieces. Then with the tip of a sharp knife, score what was the inside in a crisscross pattern, keeping the scoring as close together as possible, but do not cut all the way through. Place the squid pieces in the marinade. Cover and leave at room temperature for about 20 minutes, turning once or twice. Remove and wipe off the marinade with kitchen paper.

3. Heat the **vegetable oil** in a large frying pan over a high heat until almost smoking. Put in the squid pieces, scored-side down. Cook for 1 minute, then turn over and cook for another minute. The squid will roll up when it's ready. Remove and keep warm.

4. Heat the marinade in the frying pan until boiling, then return the squid and toss briefly to glaze. Serve on **frisée lettuce or other salad greens.**

More ideas: instead of salad leaves, serve with steamed pak choi drizzled with a little soy sauce; if you like them, you can also use the tentacles – cook for 30 seconds longer than the tubes.

15 minutes
prep

10 minutes
cook

Mussels are a great option for a quick lunch. The classic French *moules marinières* are very good, but it's nice to have something a little different.

Mussels with a kick

Store Cupboard

1 tbsp vegetable oil

2.5cm/1in root ginger, peeled and grated

2 garlic cloves, peeled and finely sliced

100ml/3½fl oz mirin or dry sherry

2 tbsp Thai fish sauce (nam pla)

juice of 1 lime

1 tsp runny honey

basmati or fragrant rice, for serving (optional)

Shopping List

2kg/4½lb cleaned mussels

1 hot red chilli, sliced

2 tbsp roughly chopped coriander, plus extra for garnishing

crusty bread, for serving (optional)

1. Discard any broken **mussels** or any that do not close when tapped against the sink before you cook them. Rinse them thoroughly in cold running water and pull off any beards.

2. Put the **vegetable oil** in a large saucepan over a medium heat, add the **chilli, ginger** and **garlic** and cook for 1 minute. Add the **mirin or sherry** and bring to the boil, then add the mussels, cover with a lid and give the pan a shake. Cook over a fierce heat for 3–5 minutes, shaking occasionally, until the mussels open. Stir in the **fish sauce, lime juice, honey** and **coriander.**

3. Discard any mussels that haven't opened. Garnish with a little extra chopped coriander and serve with **freshly cooked rice or crusty bread**.

More ideas: add a tin of coconut milk at the end and bring to simmering point before serving.

10 minutes
prep

20 minutes
cook

Another store-cupboard lunch because I'm happy to use tinned Alaskan crab for this omelette. It's an excellent product with all the taste of the sea. If you've got access to fresh-picked crab, by all means use it, but please don't use frozen.

A crab and noodle omelette

Store Cupboard

150g/5½oz rice noodles
8 large eggs
1 tbsp Thai fish sauce (nam pla)
1cm/½in root ginger, peeled and grated
vegetable oil
170g/6oz tin white crabmeat, drained

Shopping List

1 hot red chilli, finely chopped
1 tbsp finely chopped coriander
4 spring onions, thinly sliced

1. Place the **rice noodles** in a heatproof bowl, cover with boiling water and soak for a few minutes until soft, then drain, rinse in cold water and set aside.

2. Beat together the **eggs, chilli, fish sauce, coriander** and **ginger.** Set aside until ready to cook. Heat 2 tbsp **vegetable oil** in a frying pan, then add the **spring onions** and cook for 3 minutes over a medium heat before adding the **crabmeat.** Warm through and set aside.

3. To make the omelette, put 1 tsp **vegetable oil** in an omelette pan over a medium heat, then add a quarter of the noodles and warm through. Pour in a quarter of the egg mixture and cook, dragging in the edges to the middle with a wooden spoon, always keeping the eggs moving, until set underneath. Place a quarter of the crab mixture in the centre of the omelette, fold or roll the omelette and turn out onto a warm plate. Repeat 3 times to make the remaining omelettes.

Anthony's tip: don't overbeat the eggs for the omelette. You need to keep some viscosity to produce a fluffy omelette.

More ideas: cooked prawns or cooked chicken could replace the crab; add a sprinkling of finely sliced red pepper or cooked peas to make a more substantial omelette.

5 minutes
prep

25 minutes
cook

QUICK
& EASY

Scrambled eggs are highly underrated. At breakfast, lunch
or supper they satisfy most hungers. Here I've added a
Middle Eastern twist with a little help from Morecambe Bay.

Roast peppers with spiced scrambled eggs and shrimps

1. Preheat the oven to 200°C/400°F/Gas 6. Remove any seeds from the
red peppers. Place them on a roasting tray, drizzle with 2 tbsp **olive oil** and season. Place in the oven and roast for 25 minutes.

2. In the last 10 minutes before the peppers finish cooking, put the
saffron, butter, cumin and **cream** in a saucepan and bring to the
boil, then reduce the heat and simmer for 5 minutes. Add the
coriander, mint, chilli and **potted shrimps.** Allow the butter on the
shrimps to melt, then pour in the **eggs** and, stirring constantly, cook
until soft set. Immediately spoon the egg mixture into the cavity of the
peppers and serve with a **green salad.**

Antony's tip: keep an eye on the peppers while they're roasting; they
need to be soft, but must not collapse.

More ideas: instead of potted shrimps, flake in a couple of fillets of hot
smoked salmon.

Store Cupboard

extra-virgin olive oil
salt and ground black
  pepper
$1/2$ tsp saffron stamens
55g/2oz unsalted butter
$1/2$ tsp ground cumin
8 large eggs, beaten

Shopping List

4 small red peppers,
  halved through the stalk
150ml/$1/4$pt double cream
$1/2$ tbsp finely chopped
  coriander
$1/2$ tbsp finely chopped
  mint
1 mild green chilli,
  finely chopped
2 small tubs potted brown
  shrimps
green salad, for serving

Vegetarian or not, there are times when I want a vegetable salad brimming with texture, flavour and colours that appeal to the hungry eye.

Vietnamese crunchy vegetable salad

Store Cupboard

3 limes, 1 cut into wedges

3 tbsp sweet chilli sauce

3 tbsp Thai fish sauce (nam pla)

1 tbsp runny honey

2.5cm/1in root ginger, peeled and grated

Shopping List

4 carrots, peeled and shredded

½ bunch radishes, topped and tailed and quartered

¼ white cabbage, finely shredded

2 tbsp finely chopped mint

2 tbsp roughly chopped coriander

2 tbsp roughly chopped roasted peanuts

1. Squeeze the juice from **2 limes** into a bowl. Cut the **remaining lime** into 4 wedges and set aside. Add the **sweet chilli sauce, fish sauce** and **honey** to the lime juice and stir to combine.

2. In a large bowl, toss together the **carrots, radishes, cabbage, ginger, mint** and **coriander.** Add enough chilli dressing to coat the vegetables. Divide the salad between 4 plates and scatter over the **peanuts.** Serve with the lime wedges.

Antony's tip: add the dressing to the vegetable salad at the last minute to prevent discolouration.

More ideas: this salad is a great base for all sorts of protein – sashimi, cooked salmon, cooked chicken, rare beef, grilled prawns or scallops.

15 minutes
prep

5 minutes
cook

QUICK
& EASY

It's always great to find something to nibble in the fridge and it is a bonus when it's healthy and tastes good.

Flatbreads, cucumber, radishes and two dips

1. To make the curried mango dip, whisk together the **cream cheese, mango chutney, curry paste** and **half the lemon juice.** Season.

2. To make the Middle Eastern spiced yoghurt dip, put the **Greek yoghurt**, the **remaining lemon juice, tahini, cumin, paprika** and **garlic** in a food processor and blend until smooth. Season. Place in a serving bowl and drizzle with **olive oil.**

3. Heat the **flatbreads or pittas** in the oven (140°C/275°F/Gas 1) or a warm ridged griddle pan for a couple of minutes. Arrange on a large platter with the 2 dips and a bowl of **cucumber sticks, radishes** and **chicory leaves.**

More ideas: have fun by changing the veg – try spring onions, baby carrots, sliced peppers, celery sticks, baby sweetcorn, cauliflower florets, mangetout and sugar snap peas.

Store Cupboard
4 tbsp mango chutney
1 tbsp Indian curry paste
juice of 2 lemons
salt and ground black pepper
125ml/4fl oz tahini
1½ tsp ground cumin
1 tsp smoked paprika
2 garlic cloves, peeled and roughly chopped
extra-virgin olive oil

Shopping List
225g/8oz cream cheese
300 ml/½pt Greek yoghurt
8 flatbreads or pitta breads
½ cucumber, seeded and cut into sticks
1 bunch radishes, washed
chicory leaves, washed

Morocco is a fab destination. It has beautiful villas and architecture and a lot of exciting food. This dish is inspired by Zahlouk, but I've added a few extras...

Moroccan salad

1. Preheat the oven to 200°C /400°F/Gas 6. Place the **aubergines**, **courgettes**, **onion wedges** and **tomatoes** in a roasting tray and drizzle all the vegetables with the **olive oil**.

2. Roast in the oven for 35 minutes, then remove. When the vegetables are cool enough to handle, cut the aubergines in half lengthways and scoop out the flesh into a bowl.

3. Roughly chop the courgettes (which will be very soft) and add with the roast onions to the aubergine flesh. Peel the tomatoes, discard the skin and roughly chop the flesh and pulp.

4. In a frying pan, heat the olive oil from the roasting tray. Add the **garlic** and fry until it starts to colour. Add the **harissa** and **cumin seeds** and stir-fry for 2 minutes. Add the chopped tomato and cook until reduced to a pulp. Then add the vegetable mixture along with the **chickpeas**, **lemon juice** and **coriander**.

5. Toss together to combine. Season and serve the salad warm or at room temperature with **flatbread** and a dollop of **yoghurt**.

More ideas: add a sliced red pepper to the roast veg; substitute rinsed, drained white beans for the chickpeas.

Store Cupboard

1 onion, cut into 8 wedges

1 red onion, cut into 8 wedges

85ml/3fl oz extra-virgin olive oil

4 garlic cloves, peeled and crushed

2 tsp harissa

1 tsp cumin seeds

400g/14oz tin chickpeas, rinsed and drained

juice of 1 lemon

salt and ground black pepper

Shopping List

2 medium aubergines

2 courgettes

2 beefsteak tomatoes

1 bunch coriander, roughly chopped

flatbread, for serving

natural yoghurt, for serving

If you grow your own peas and broad beans this salad will be even more delicious. It's lovely on its own or it goes very well with grilled meat or fish.

Spring vegetable and feta salad

Store Cupboard

grated zest and juice of
 1 lemon

pinch of chilli flakes

60ml/2fl oz extra-virgin
 olive oil

salt and ground black
 pepper

Shopping List

115g/4oz peas, fresh or
 frozen

115g/4oz broad beans,
 fresh or frozen

20 mint leaves, shredded

2 spring onions, finely
 sliced

115g/4oz good-quality feta

1. Small and fresh **peas** and **broad beans** don't need to be cooked. If large or frozen, cook them in boiling salted water for 3 minutes, drain and refresh under cold water, then drain again. Mix the peas and beans with the **mint, spring onions, lemon zest** and **chilli flakes.** Toss to combine, then add the **olive oil** and **lemon juice.** Season and arrange in a bowl.

2. Push the **feta** through a fine sieve over the salad to create a snow-like effect.

Antony's tip: some chefs like to double pod the broad beans – peel off the leathery skin that surrounds each bean – but this is only necessary if the beans are large and old.

More ideas: dice half an avocado for a great addition; serve with Serrano or Parma ham.

Scallops, bacon and black pudding – three of my favourite ingredients – go really well together in a salad. They are not the cheapest of raw materials, but we all need a little treat.

Some of my favourite flavours in a salad

Store Cupboard

1 tbsp olive oil

2 tbsp walnut oil

1 tbsp sherry vinegar

salt and ground black
  pepper

Shopping List

6 shallots, half finely diced
  and half finely sliced

225g/8oz mixed crunchy
  salad leaves

175g/6oz smoked streaky
  bacon rashers, diced

175g/6oz black pudding,
  cut into 1cm/½in slices

8 cleaned diver-caught
  scallops, sliced in half
  (including the corals)

1. Combine the **diced shallots** and **salad leaves.**

2. Heat the **olive oil** in a large frying pan. Add the **bacon** and cook over a medium heat until nearly crispy (about 3 minutes) before adding the **black pudding.** Cook for about 5 minutes, turning once, until the pudding is crispy. Remove the bacon and black pudding and keep warm.

3. Add the **sliced shallots** and **scallops** to the hot frying pan. Cook the scallops for 1 minute each side until golden but still opaque in the centre. Return the bacon and black pudding to the pan with the **walnut oil** and **vinegar.** Toss to combine, then pour over the salad, tossing again. Season and serve.

Antony's tip: it's important to buy diver-caught scallops if you want them to have a golden crust. Frozen scallops contain too much water and boil rather than fry.

More ideas: substitute raw prawns for scallops; chorizo sausage makes a good alternative to black pudding.

10 minutes
prep

8 minutes
cook

Deep-fried Camembert was always a retro classic – Ed Baines inspired me when he did a similar dish on *Daily Cooks Challenge*. It's lovely and easy. He did it in five minutes, but it might take you a little longer.

Deep-fried almond-coated Brie, apple and pear salad

Store Cupboard

115g/4oz plain flour
2 large eggs, beaten
25g/1oz ground almonds
25g/1oz soft white
 breadcrumbs
1 tbsp apple sauce
1 tsp wholegrain mustard
extra-virgin olive oil
juice of 1 lemon
salt and ground black
 pepper

Shopping List

300g/10½oz Brie, cut into
 4 equal wedges
1 Cox's apple
1 Conference pear
2 handfuls of rocket leaves

1. Place the **flour** on a plate, the **beaten eggs** on another and combine the **almonds** and **breadcrumbs** on a third plate. Dip the **Brie wedges** in the flour, followed by the egg, followed by the almond mixture. Make sure they're well coated. Set aside in the fridge until ready to fry.

2. To make the dressing, mix together the **apple sauce, mustard**, 125ml/4fl oz **olive oil** and the **lemon juice**. Season.

3. Core the **apple** and **pear** and then slice into thin slivers. Arrange the **rocket** on 4 plates, top with the apples and pears and drizzle with the apple dressing.

4. Heat 2 tbsp **olive oil** in a large frying pan over a medium heat, put in the Brie and brown on all sides for about 6–8 minutes, turning carefully with tongs. You can't afford to leave the Brie because it burns very easily. Arrange the Brie on top of the salad and serve immediately.

More ideas: try adding 2 tbsp crushed walnuts to the breadcrumbs for a more adult coating to the Brie; add some walnut halves to the salad.

You can't get much easier than this; a fresh-tasting pasta dish that takes no time at all.

Fresh and green spaghetti

1. Bring a large pan of salted water to the boil, then gradually ease the **spaghetti** into the water. Stir for 2 minutes to prevent the spaghetti sticking together. Cook the pasta for 1 minute less than the manufacturer's instructions.

2. Meanwhile, in a large frying pan over a medium heat, melt the **butter** until foaming. Add the **peas** and **courgettes** and cook gently without colouring for 3 minutes. Add the **basil.** Toss to combine, season and remove from the heat.

3. Drain the pasta and immediately tip it onto the vegetables with the water still clinging to it. Squeeze over the **lemon juice** and scatter with the **Parmesan.** Toss to combine and finish with a splash of **olive oil.** Serve immediately.

Antony's tip: I cook the pasta less than the manufacturer's instructions because I want it firmer than al dente. How the pasta is cooked is up to you, but please don't overcook it.

More ideas: try some grilled artichokes (from a jar), roughly chopped and added towards the end with the basil.

Store Cupboard
280g/10oz dried spaghetti
55g/2oz unsalted butter
salt and ground black pepper
juice of 1 lemon
25g/1oz Parmesan, freshly grated
extra-virgin olive oil

Shopping List
115g/4oz peas, fresh or frozen
2 courgettes, thinly sliced
½ bunch basil, leaves shredded

10 minutes
prep

20 minutes
cook

QUICK
& EASY

Creamed spinach is one of my favourite vegetables and why shouldn't it work with pasta? I like this combo, but I have to admit I've never seen it in the Italian culinary repertoire.

A very green bowl of pasta

1. Preheat the oven to 200°C/400°F/Gas 6. Place the **tomato wedges** in a roasting tray, drizzle with 2 tbsp **olive oil,** season and sprinkle with the **thyme** and **half the garlic.** Place in the oven and cook until the tomatoes are just starting to collapse (about 15 minutes).

2. Meanwhile, heat a large saucepan with the **butter.** When foaming, add the **onion** and **remaining garlic** and cook for 5 minutes over a medium heat, stirring from time to time, then add the **spinach** and cook until wilted. Drain in a colander with the onion and garlic, pushing down to squeeze out the water. Put the spinach mixture in a food processor with the **cream** and **nutmeg** and blitz until smooth. Return to the saucepan and season to taste.

3. At the same time, cook the **fettuccine or tagliatelle** in a large pan of boiling salted water, stirring for the first 2 minutes to prevent it sticking together, until al dente, about 1 minute less than the manufacturer's instructions. Drain and fold into the spinach cream.

4. Divide the pasta between 4 warm bowls, arrange the roast tomatoes in the centre and top with **Parmesan shavings** and a drizzle of **olive oil.**

Store Cupboard

olive oil

salt and ground black pepper

4 garlic cloves, peeled and finely chopped

40g/1½oz unsalted butter

1 onion, finely chopped

¼ tsp grated nutmeg

55g/2oz Parmesan, shaved

Shopping List

4 plum tomatoes, each cut into 6 wedges

1 tsp thyme leaves

500g/1lb 2oz spinach, tough stalks removed and washed

150ml/¼pt double cream

500g/1lb 2oz dried spinach fettuccine or tagliatelle

15 minutes
prep

40 minutes
cook

This recipe has its roots in vichyssoise, a cold soup, but this is one to have in bed or in front of a roaring fire. It'll warm every part of your body. It's also what I call a flask soup, that is, one to take to work.

A winter warming bowl of goodness

Store Cupboard

55g/2oz unsalted butter

2 onions, sliced

450g/1lb floury potatoes, e.g. Maris Piper, Mayan Gold or King Edward

900ml/1½pt vegetable stock

2 bay leaves

Shopping List

225g/8oz leeks, white part only, shredded

150ml/¼pt double cream

1 small bunch chives, snipped

crusty bread, for serving

1. Melt the **butter** in a large saucepan over a medium heat. Add the **leeks** and **onions.** Cook over a very gentle heat for 20 minutes, stirring occasionally so that the onion doesn't colour. Meanwhile, peel and dice the **potatoes.**

2. Throw the potatoes into the pan with the leeks and onions, stir, then add the **stock** and **bay leaves.** Cover with a lid and simmer for 15 minutes until the potatoes are tender and starting to break down. Remove the bay leaves and blend until smooth in a food processor or liquidizer. Return the soup to the saucepan, stir in the **cream** and **chives** and gently heat. Serve with **crusty bread.**

Antony's tip: I've discovered this great potato called Mayan Gold, which is originally from Peru, but is now grown in the UK. It hates water, so is perfect for roasting and chips, and is brilliant in soup, as it breaks down on its own. It's also perfect for Irish stew because the potato thickens the sauce.

More ideas: some crispy bacon pieces or fried onion rings scattered over the top is delicious.

10 minutes
prep

20 minutes
cook

QUICK
& EASY

Vegetarian food has a lot to offer. These fritters are a reasonably healthy snack and are an exciting accompaniment to a roast or a grill.

Cauliflower and courgette fritters with a Gorgonzola dip

1. Drop the **cauliflower florets** into a saucepan of boiling salted water and cook until tender (about 5 minutes). Drain and place in a bowl, then roughly chop.

2. Place the **grated courgette** in a clean tea towel and squeeze dry. Add to the cauliflower and toss to combine.

3. Sift the **flour, baking powder** and **cayenne** into a bowl. Make a well in the centre and crack in the **eggs.** Mix with a wooden spoon until almost smooth, then season. Add the **Gruyère** and **Parmesan** to the batter together with the cauliflower and courgette mixture and mix well.

4. Heat the **vegetable oil** to 170°C/325°F preferably in a deep-fat-fryer, or in a heavy-based saucepan. The oil should be at least 2.5cm/1in deep.

5. While the oil is warming up, put the **Gorgonzola** and **soured cream** in a mini food processor and whiz until smooth.

6. Carefully drop 4 individual tablespoonfuls of the cauliflower and courgette batter into the fat, using another spoon to push the mixture off, and fry until golden brown turning them as necessary (about 3–4 minutes). Remove and drain on kitchen paper. Keep warm while you cook the remaining fritters. This recipe should make about 16 fritters. Serve immediately with the Gorgonzola dip.

Store Cupboard

55g/2oz plain flour

1 tsp baking powder

½ tsp cayenne pepper

2 large eggs

salt and ground black pepper

15g/½oz Parmesan, freshly grated

vegetable oil, for deep-frying

Shopping List

½ cauliflower, cut into florets

1 large courgette, topped, tailed and grated

55g/2oz Gruyère, grated

115g/4oz Gorgonzola, cubed

150ml/¼pt soured cream

This recipe is one for the mother-in-law, a really quick soup to knock up and impress. A good all-rounder, you can serve it for lunch, a snack or as a dinner party starter.

Pea and spinach soup with horseradish cream

Store Cupboard

2 tbsp olive oil

2 garlic cloves, peeled
and sliced

900ml/1½pt vegetable or
chicken stock

3 tbsp horseradish sauce

salt and ground white
pepper

1 tsp caster sugar

Shopping List

1 bunch spring onions,
roughly chopped

450g/1lb peas, fresh or
frozen

150ml/¼pt double cream

250g bag baby spinach,
washed

1. Heat the **olive oil** in a saucepan over a low heat. Add the **spring onions** and **garlic** and cook gently for 8 minutes, stirring from time to time. Add the **stock** and bring to the boil, then add the **peas** and boil for 3 minutes.

2. Meanwhile, whip **half the cream** with an electric hand whisk to soft peaks, then fold in the **horseradish sauce.** Season with **salt and ground white pepper.** Set aside.

3. Add the **spinach** and **sugar** to the soup and cook until the spinach has wilted. Ladle the soup into a food processor or liquidizer and blend until smooth, then return to the saucepan. Add the **remaining cream**, season and gently heat. Ladle into 4 warm bowls and float a spoonful of the horseradish cream on the surface.

Antony's tip: for a more professional finish, you can pass the soup through a fine sieve, but personally I don't mind a little texture.

More ideas: replace the spinach with watercress.

Dinner

One-pot suppers are always pleasing cold weather fare. This super-easy dish has Puy lentils packed full of goodness plus the comfort of good, hearty sausages.

A thrifty lentil supper

Store Cupboard

1 tbsp olive oil

1 onion, finely diced

2 garlic cloves, peeled and finely chopped

1 bay leaf

½ tsp dried thyme

175ml/6fl oz red wine

225g/8oz Puy lentils

450m/16fl oz chicken stock

salt and ground black pepper

Shopping List

6 sausages, your favourite

4 dry-cured streaky bacon rashers, rinds removed and roughly chopped

175g/6oz field (Portobello) mushrooms, thickly sliced

1 tbsp roughly chopped parsley

1. Put the **olive oil** in a large saucepan over a medium heat. Brown the **sausages** all over, but do not cook through. Remove and cut into 2.5cm/1in pieces.

2. Add the **onion, garlic** and **bacon** and fry until the onion has softened and the bacon has crisped (about 8 minutes). Stir in the **mushrooms, bay leaf, thyme** and **wine.** Allow the wine to boil, then when it has all bubbled away, add the **lentils** and **stock.**

3. Simmer uncovered for 25 minutes, topping up with extra stock if necessary. The lentil mixture should have a soupy consistency, rather like risotto. In the last 10 minutes of cooking, return the sausages to the pan.

4. Season and sprinkle over the **parsley**. Heat through and serve.

More ideas: replace your favourite sausages with chorizo sausage and/or black pudding.

Most modern breeds of pig end up far too lean and their pork often tastes of dry cardboard because most people overcook it. Here's a way of getting loads of flavour, but also keeping it succulent.

Pork chops with Chinese flavours

Store Cupboard

2 tbsp runny honey

2 tbsp ketjap manis (see tip opposite)

2 tbsp hoisin sauce

2 tsp sesame oil

2.5cm/1in root ginger, peeled and grated

2 garlic cloves, peeled and crushed

Maldon sea salt

1 tbsp vegetable oil

Shopping List

4 thick pork chops, rinds removed

1 cucumber, peeled, seeded and cut into batons

6 spring onions, shredded into fine strips

boiled new potatoes, for serving

1. Put the **honey, ketjap manis, hoisin sauce, sesame oil** and **ginger** in a flat dish and stir to combine. Take the **crushed garlic** and a little **salt** and with the back of a knife crush them together into a paste, then add to the marinade.

2. Place the **pork chops** in the marinade and make sure they're well coated. Cover and leave in the fridge for as long as you can, preferably overnight but for at least 3 hours.

3. Heat a large frying pan with the **vegetable oil.** Clean most of the marinade from the chops with kitchen paper and fry them over a medium heat for 4 minutes each side, regularly spooning over the marinade and turning to glaze them, until cooked through. Be careful, as this marinade burns easily.

4. Place the chops on 4 warm plates, then scatter over the **cucumber** and **spring onions.** Serve with **new potatoes.**

Antony's tip: if you're worried about burning the chops, put them in an oven preheated to 180°C/350°F/Gas 4 for 12 minutes until cooked through, basting regularly.

More ideas: substitute 700g/1lb 9oz diced pork fillet for the pork chops.

15 minutes
prep

45 minutes
cook

SLOW
& EASY

These pork escalopes are just pork, plain and simple. I'm not doing anything to it. But the butternut, now you're talking. This is a really exciting vegetable dish.

Pork escalopes with spicy butternut

1. Preheat the oven to 200°C/400°F/Gas 6. Cut the **butternut squash** in half lengthways and remove the seeds. Cut each half lengthways into 4 wedges, then cut each wedge in half crossways. Place the squash in a roasting tin, season and drizzle with **2 tbsp vegetable oil.** Roast in the oven, turning the squash over from time to time, until soft and caramelized (about 35 minutes).

2. Meanwhile, put the **chillies, garlic, cumin, ground and fresh coriander, vinegar** and **sugar** in a saucepan. Bring to the boil, then reduce the heat and simmer until the liquid becomes syrupy (about 6 minutes). Transfer to a flat dish and stir in the **ketjap manis** and **sesame oil.** Place the **pork** in this mixture, cover and leave to marinate while the butternut is cooking.

3. In the last 10 minutes before the butternut finishes cooking, heat a large frying pan with **the remaining vegetable oil.** Remove the pork from the marinade and fry for 3 minutes each side until cooked through.

4. Remove the squash from the oven and pour over the marinade. Return to the oven and roast for a further 10 minutes, basting regularly. Serve the pork with the butternut and any juices.

Antony's tip: ketjap manis is an Indonesian sweet soy sauce. If you have difficulty finding it, just use soy sauce mixed with 1 tbsp soft brown sugar.

Store Cupboard

salt and ground black pepper

3 tbsp vegetable oil

2 garlic cloves, peeled and crushed

1 tsp ground cumin

1 tsp ground coriander

6 tbsp rice vinegar

2 tbsp soft dark brown sugar

3 tbsp ketjap manis (see tip below)

2 tsp sesame oil

Shopping List

1 medium butternut squash

2 hot red chillies, roughly chopped

4 x 175g/6oz pork escalopes or boneless chop steaks

3 tbsp roughly chopped coriander

This is really a basic construction job, with everything stuffed into individual roasting bags. Prepare on Sunday, eat Monday night: simplicity itself.

Supper in a bag

1. Lay out 4 roasting bags flat on a work surface and divide the **onion** and **garlic** between them. On top of the onion, arrange each **sliced chicken breast** into its original shape. Insert a slice of **chorizo** between each slice of chicken, then place a **thyme sprig** on top of the chicken. Top the thyme with a **bacon rasher.**

2. In a bowl, combine the **flageolet beans, tomatoes** and **wine** and season. Spoon this mixture around the chicken. Seal the bags and refrigerate, making sure you keep them flat, for up to 3 days until ready to cook.

3. Preheat the oven to 200°C/400°F/Gas 6. Put the bags on a baking tray and cook for 20–25 minutes or until the chicken is cooked through. Give each person a bag and offer **Greek yoghurt** to spoon on top.

More ideas: substitute sliced new potatoes or rinsed and drained butter beans for the flageolet beans; use boneless, skinless chicken thighs instead of breasts.

Store Cupboard

1 onion, finely sliced

3 garlic cloves, peeled and finely sliced

400g/14oz tin flageolet beans, rinsed and drained

400g/14oz tin chopped tomatoes

175ml/6fl oz dry white wine

salt and ground black pepper

Shopping List

4 boneless, skinless chicken breasts each sliced in 4 widthways

12 slices chorizo sausage

4 thyme sprigs

4 smoked back bacon rashers, rinds removed

100g/3½oz Greek yoghurt, for serving

I wanted to give you some risotto recipes, but I'm not sure a good risotto is that easy to make. However a pilaf is fairly foolproof and it has loads of interesting flavours.

Lamb pilaf

Store Cupboard

1 tbsp vegetable oil

1 onion, finely chopped

2 garlic cloves, peeled and finely chopped

2.5cm/1in root ginger, peeled and grated

2 tsp ground coriander

1 tsp ground cumin

1 tsp ground turmeric

2 cardamom pods, cracked

300g/10½oz long-grain rice, such as Uncle Ben's

55g/2oz unsalted butter

750ml/1¼pt chicken stock or water

juice of 1 lemon

salt and ground black pepper

Shopping List

325g/12oz lamb mince

1 hot green chilli, finely chopped

115g/4oz peas, fresh or frozen

2 tbsp finely chopped coriander

1. Preheat the oven to 180°C/350°F/Gas 4.

2. Put the **vegetable oil** in an ovenproof saucepan and fry the **lamb mince, onion, garlic** and **ginger** over a medium heat for 8 minutes, stirring regularly, until the lamb is browned and the onion golden. Add **all the spices** and **chilli** and stir to combine, then add the **peas, rice** and **butter.** Cook for 1 minute, stirring to mix the flavours. Add the **chicken stock or water** and bring to the boil. Cover with greaseproof paper and a tightly fitting lid and pop in the oven for 10 minutes.

3. Remove from the oven and leave to rest for 5 minutes. Take off the lid and paper and fluff up the pilaf with a fork. Stir in the **lemon juice** and **chopped coriander.** Check the seasoning.

Antony's tip: cook this on the hob following the same principles of paper and lid, using the same cooking time over a medium heat, but don't be nosey and don't fiddle with it.

More ideas: use diced meat instead of mince as long as it's a tender cut, such as leg; a dollop of yoghurt and some toasted almonds make a nice garnish.

This is a fairly dry stir-fry and it is very fast, so it's important to use tender lamb from the cutlet, leg or fillet.

An Anglified look at stir-fried lamb

Store Cupboard

1 tbsp vegetable oil

4 garlic cloves, peeled and finely chopped

90ml/3fl oz oyster sauce

3 tbsp light soy sauce

2 tsp soft dark brown sugar

long-grain or basmati rice, for serving

Shopping List

675g/1½lb lamb fillet, thinly sliced

2 hot red chillies, thinly sliced

225g/8oz tenderstem broccoli, trimmed and cut into chunks

1 bunch mint, three-quarters finely chopped, quarter leaves

handful of beansprouts

1. Put a wok over a high heat and add the **vegetable oil.** When hot, add **a little lamb** and **a little garlic** and stir-fry vigorously for about 2 minutes, remove and set aside. Repeat with the **remaining lamb** and **garlic**.

2. Once all the lamb is out of the pan, add the **chilli, broccoli, oyster sauce** and **soy sauce** and stir-fry for 3 minutes. Return the lamb to the wok together with the **sugar, chopped mint** and **mint leaves** and cook for another 2 minutes. Finally, add the **beansprouts** and cook for 30 seconds. Serve immediately with freshly cooked **rice.**

More Ideas: a handful of roughly chopped cashew nuts make a nice textural topping.

A good curry involves a fair few spices, that's the name of the game. This recipe has a lot of ingredients but your well-stocked store cupboard should contain many of them, so there's very little to buy.

A lamb curry in the style of rogan josh

1. If there's time, soak the **lamb** in cold water for 15–30 minutes; this makes the meat paler. Drain.

2. Heat the **vegetable oil** in a large saucepan. Add the **onion** and **garlic** and cook over a medium heat until the onion has softened (about 7 minutes). Stir in the **yoghurt, chilli powder, ground coriander, cloves, cumin, cardamom, turmeric, ginger, tinned tomatoes** and **salt.** Bring to the boil, then reduce the heat and simmer for 5 minutes.

3. Add the soaked lamb and cook over a gentle heat, stirring from time to time, until the lamb is tender and cooked through (about 1¾ hours). Add the **tomato wedges** and cook for 10 minutes, then stir in the **garam masala.**

4. Sprinkle with the **flaked almonds** and **fresh coriander** and serve with **basmati rice.**

Antony's tip: I use Greek yoghurt because as it's a strained yoghurt the sauce is less likely to split (separate).

More ideas: I like to add a couple of handfuls of baby spinach to the curry just before the end of cooking; you can also try root vegetables such as sweet potato and carrots or green vegetables such as broccoli, peas and sugar snap peas.

Store Cupboard

1 tbsp vegetable oil
2 onions, finely chopped
4 garlic cloves, peeled and crushed
1 tsp chilli powder
1 tbsp ground coriander
2 cloves
2 tsp ground cumin
1 tsp ground cardamom
1 tsp ground turmeric
5cm/2in root ginger, peeled and grated
400g/14oz tin chopped tomatoes
1 tsp salt
1 tsp garam masala
25g/1oz toasted flaked almonds
basmati rice, for serving

Shopping List

1kg/2lb 4oz diced lamb
125g/4½oz Greek yoghurt
3 tomatoes, each cut into 4 wedges
1 tbsp roughly chopped coriander

This is really good and really easy and uses just a couple of pans. And it has lots of garlicky Mediterranean flavours.

Leg of lamb steaks with roast tomatoes and courgettes

1. Preheat the oven to 200°C/400°F/Gas 6. Place a roasting tray on the hob over a medium heat. Add 100ml/3½fl oz **olive oil** and the **potatoes**, season and toss them around in the tin to start the browning process, then pop them in the oven for 15 minutes.

2. Meanwhile, boil a pan of water. Make a shallow cross in the top and bottom of the **tomatoes**. Plunge them into the boiling water for 30 seconds, remove and peel.

3. Cut each tomato into 6 wedges and add to the potatoes in the roasting tray with the **courgettes, garlic** and **thyme** and roast for another 25 minutes.

4. Meanwhile, heat a large frying pan or ridged griddle pan. Season the **lamb steaks** well and drizzle with 2 tbsp **olive oil.** Fry over a fierce heat until nicely coloured, then reduce the heat and cook for 3 minutes each side until cooked through. Allow to rest in a warm place for 10 minutes.

5. Remove the roast vegetables from the oven and toss with the **vinegar.** Serve with the lamb steaks.

Antony's tip: I prefer to skin the tomatoes but feel free not to.

More ideas: the roast vegetables also go very well with grilled fish.

Store Cupboard
extra-virgin olive oil
16 waxy salad potatoes, e.g. Charlotte or Pink Fir, scrubbed and quartered lengthways
salt and ground black pepper
12 garlic cloves, peeled
1 tbsp balsamic vinegar

Shopping List
4 beefsteak or Jack Hawkins tomatoes
4 courgettes, each cut into 5cm x 2.5cm/2in x 1in chunks
4 thyme sprigs
4 leg of lamb steaks (about 300g/10½oz each)

This is reminiscent of the *souvlakia* you get in Greece: the flavours work, the salad is healthy, it's a holiday on a plate.

Marinated lamb on a Greek salad

Store Cupboard

4 garlic cloves, peeled and crushed to a paste with a little salt

grated zest and juice of 2 lemons

1 tsp ground cumin

1 tsp ground coriander

6 tbsp extra-virgin olive oil

Maldon sea salt and ground black pepper

Shopping List

3 tsp dried wild oregano

675g/1½lb leg of lamb, cubed

4 tomatoes, roughly chopped

½ cucumber, peeled, seeded and roughly chopped

55g/2oz Kalamata olives

115g/4oz good feta, diced

1. Combine the **garlic paste, half the oregano, zest of 2 lemons and juice of 1 lemon, cumin, coriander** and **3 tbsp olive oil.** Add the **cubes of lamb** to this marinade and toss to combine. Cover and leave to marinate for a minimum of 1 hour in the fridge, but overnight if possible.

2. Combine the **tomatoes, cucumber, olives, feta** and **remaining oregano.** Season with **salt and ground black pepper.**

3. Heat a ridged griddle pan over a fierce heat and cook the lamb and marinade to brown the meat and evaporate the liquid, then reduce the heat and cook for 6–8 minutes until the meat is cooked through.

4. Dress the Greek salad with **the remaining olive oil** and the **juice of 1 lemon.** Season. Arrange the salad on 4 plates and place the cooked lamb on top of the salad.

More ideas: arrange the meat on skewers for a more formal presentation; minced, this lamb mixture is good in a flatbread or pitta with a dollop of yoghurt or hummus and some crunchy salad.

This is one of the first Italian dishes I learnt while working in the Adriatico restaurant in Woodford Green, oh so many years ago. That recipe didn't include the bacon, but I like it.

Calf's liver, bacon and sage

Store Cupboard

2 tbsp plain flour

salt and ground black pepper

85g/3oz unsalted butter

2 tbsp olive oil

juice of ½ lemon

good splash of white wine

Shopping List

450g/1lb calf's liver, cut into 8 slices

4 dry-cured back bacon rashers, rinds removed and roughly chopped

2 tbsp finely chopped sage

lyonnaise potatoes, for serving (see p.185)

1. Sprinkle the **flour** onto a flat plate and season. Coat both sides of the **liver** in flour and pat to remove any excess. Melt **55g/2oz butter** and the **olive oil** in a large frying pan and when the butter is foaming add half the liver and cook over a fierce heat for 1 minute on each side until cooked through. Remove and keep warm. Repeat with the remaining liver.

2. In the same pan, melt the **remaining butter.** Add the **bacon** and **sage** and cook over a high heat until the bacon is crispy (about 4 minutes), stirring to remove any bits from the bottom of the pan. Add the **lemon juice** and **wine** and boil until thickened to a sauce. Pour over the liver and serve with lyonnaise potatoes.

Antony's tip: overcooking the liver can make it tough, so make sure your pan is really hot to cook it quickly.

More ideas: sliced lamb or veal kidneys can also be cooked this way.

This is one of those dishes that you wouldn't look at twice, but should you taste it you would change your mind. Remember, beauty is only skin deep. It's what's underneath that matters.

Rustic roast

1. Preheat the oven to 140°C/275°F/Gas 1.

2. Heat a large casserole or roasting tray on the hob with the **butter** and **olive oil.** Season the **lamb shoulder** and brown all over in the pan over a medium heat for about 8 minutes. Remove and set aside.

3. Add the **onion, garlic, thyme** and **bay leaves** to the pan and brown gently, stirring from time to time, for 8 minutes. Add the **anchovies** and **wine** and bring to the boil. Return the lamb to the casserole, seal tightly with a lid or foil and pop into the oven to cook for 3 hours.

4. Remove the pot from the oven and add the **potatoes.** Cover again and return to the oven for another 2 hours. Remove the lid, turn the heat up to 190°C/375°F/Gas 5 and cook for 20 minutes to crisp the lamb skin. Remove the lamb from the oven and leave to rest for 20 minutes. Serve the lamb with some **spring greens or broccoli**, the cooking juices and potatoes.

More ideas: try half a shoulder of pork, but discard the rind after cooking.

Store Cupboard

85g/3oz unsalted butter
50ml/2fl oz olive oil
salt and ground black pepper
4 onions, each cut into 6
15 garlic cloves, peeled
2 bay leaves
6 anchovy fillets in oil
450ml/16fl oz white wine
6 floury potatoes, e.g Maris Piper or King Edward, scrubbed and each cut into 4

Shopping List

1 whole shoulder of lamb
2 thyme sprigs
spring greens or broccoli, for serving

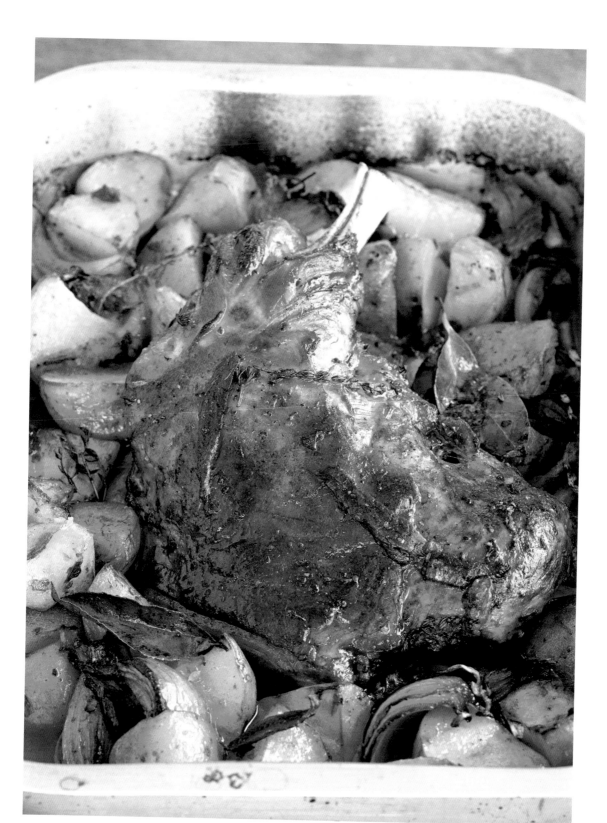

15 minutes prep
1 hour marinate

6 minutes
cook

SLOW
& EASY

No, this is not the crispy shreds of batter with a hint of beef that you get in many Chinese restaurants – this is much more delicious. I'm using fillet steak here, but you could go for rump or sirloin.

Chilli beef

1. Combine the **ketjap manis, sambal oelek or chilli, garlic, chilli powder, sugar, sesame oil** and 2 tbsp **water** in a bowl. Add the **beef** and mix well. Cover and leave to marinate in the fridge for 1 hour.

2. Heat a wok over a high heat, add 1 tbsp **vegetable oil** and swirl around to coat the wok. Add the beef and its marinade in 2–3 batches and stir-fry aggressively for 2 minutes. Remove each batch with a slotted spoon and set aside to keep warm while you cook the remaining beef.

3. Sprinkle the chilli beef with the **coriander, peanuts** and **spring onions.** Serve immediately.

Antony's tip: if you can't find ketjap manis, replace with 60ml soy sauce mixed with 1 tbsp soft dark brown sugar; when stir-frying, keep the meat moving so that you sear it on all sides; if you're not a fan of raw onion, cook it with the beef.

More ideas: this is equally good with chicken breast or pork fillet.

Store Cupboard
60ml/2fl oz ketjap manis (see tip)
2 garlic cloves, peeled and crushed
½ tsp chilli powder
1 tbsp soft dark brown sugar
1 tsp sesame oil
vegetable oil

Shopping List
1 tbsp sambal oelek or 1 hot red chilli, finely chopped
400g/14oz beef fillet, very thinly sliced
3 tbsp finely chopped coriander
2 tbsp roughly chopped roasted peanuts
4 spring onions, finely sliced

I love game. It's so healthy in comparison to many domesticated meats. Game isn't mainstream mainly because it's misunderstood. Everyone thinks it reeks of death and decomposition – it doesn't have to!

Pot-roast pheasant with cider and bacon

Store Cupboard

1 tbsp vegetable oil

85g/3oz unsalted butter

4 garlic cloves, peeled and crushed

6 juniper berries, crushed

2 bay leaves

salt and ground black pepper

Shopping List

2 hen pheasants

8 smoked dry-cured streaky bacon rashers, rinds removed

2 thyme sprigs

150ml/¼pt traditional dry cider

1 Cox's apple, peeled, cored and diced

Savoy cabbage, for serving

game chips, (see p.181) or buttery mash, for serving

1. Preheat the oven to 180°C/350°F/Gas 4. Put the **vegetable oil** and **25g/1oz butter** (put the rest in the fridge) in a large flameproof casserole over a medium heat and brown the **pheasants** all over. Remove and set aside. Then add the **bacon, garlic, thyme, juniper** and **bay leaves** to the casserole and brown the bacon. Pour in the **cider** and bring to the boil.

2. Place the pheasants on their side on one breast in the casserole, cover with a lid and cook for 15 minutes. Take out and turn the pheasants onto their other side. Baste the birds with the juices, cover and return to the oven for 10 minutes. Remove the pheasants and bacon to rest and keep warm.

3. Add the **diced apple** to the casserole and boil until the apple is tender (about 5 minutes). Cut the **remaining cold butter** into small pieces and whisk in.

4. Carve the birds and give everyone a breast and a thigh and 2 bacon rashers. Spoon over the juices and serve with **savoy cabbage** and **game chips or buttery mash.**

Antony's tip: there is no point serving the drumsticks, as there are too many sinews. Chop them up with the carcass and a few veg such as carrots, onion and celery to make a game stock.

More ideas: this recipe works well with 4 partridge. You'll need to cook them for just 16 minutes.

Rabbits are cute little animals, but then chickens can be very pretty too. Many people have a mental block when it comes to eating our furry friend, yet rabbit is widely bred to be eaten, so put your bias behind you.

Rabbit legs with roast shallots and mustard sauce

Store Cupboard

140g/5oz unsalted butter

1 tbsp olive oil

90ml/3fl oz sherry vinegar

2 tbsp Dijon mustard

1 tbsp wholegrain mustard

300ml/½pt chicken stock

1 tsp dried thyme

1 tsp smoked paprika

1 tsp dried rosemary

6 garlic cloves, peeled and crushed

salt and ground black pepper

Shopping List

8 shallots, peeled and halved through the root

4 farmed rabbit legs

150ml/¼pt double cream

mashed potato, for serving

greens, e.g. broccoli or cabbage, for serving

1. Preheat the oven to 180°C/350°F/Gas 4. Heat **55g/2oz butter** and the **olive oil** in an ovenproof frying pan. Place the **shallots**, cut-side down, in the pan and cook for 3 minutes over a medium heat to start the browning process. Pop the shallots in the oven and cook for 40 minutes, turning them after 30 minutes. Remove and keep warm.

2. Meanwhile, heat the **remaining butter** in a large flameproof casserole over a medium heat. Brown the **rabbit legs** all over. Remove and set aside. Add **all the remaining ingredients except the garlic and cream** and whisk to combine. Bring to the boil, then return the rabbit to the casserole, reduce the heat and simmer with the lid on for 40 minutes until the meat is cooked through. Remove the rabbit legs and keep warm with the shallots. Strain the cooking juices and return them to the pan. Add the **garlic** and **cream** and season to taste.

3. Bring to the boil then reduce the heat and simmer until the sauce coats the back of a spoon. Return the rabbit to the pan and heat through for about 5 minutes. Serve with the **roast shallots, mash** and some **greens.**

More ideas: if you are too squeamish to eat rabbit, don't miss out, just use chicken thighs instead.

Who doesn't like something with a little sweetness? Chicken thighs lend themselves well to this recipe and are great value.

Sticky chicken nuggets

1. **Place all the ingredients except the chicken, onion wedges and vegetable oil** in a bowl and mix together.

2. Cut the **chicken** into 2.5cm/1in pieces and add to the marinade and toss to combine. Cover with cling film and leave in the fridge overnight, or for a minimum of 3 hours.

3. Heat a large frying pan with the **vegetable oil** over a medium heat. Remove the chicken from the marinade, wiping off as much marinade as possible with kitchen paper. Add to the pan with the **onion** and fry both for 8–10 minutes until the chicken is golden. Cover with a lid, turn down the heat and cook gently for 10 minutes, stirring from time to time. Remove the lid, pour in the marinade and simmer gently, stirring constantly, for about 20 minutes until the chicken is cooked through and really sticky. Serve with **new potatoes or rice.**

More ideas: feel free to use chicken breasts, although they won't be so succulent; this also works very well with chicken wings.

Store Cupboard

1 tbsp runny honey

4 garlic cloves, peeled and crushed

2.5cm/1in root ginger, peeled and grated

4 tbsp rice vinegar

2 tbsp sweet chilli sauce

4 tbsp ketjap manis (see tip p.107)

2 tsp tomato purée

juice and grated zest of 2 limes

2 tbsp vegetable oil

2 onions, each cut into 8 wedges

long-grain rice, for serving (optional)

Shopping List

2 medium hot green chillies, finely chopped

6 boneless chicken thighs, skin on

boiled new potatoes, for serving (optional)

A real winter warmer that can be cooked in advance and reheated or microwaved, with lots of Spanish flavours.

A Mediterranean chicken casserole

Store Cupboard

olive oil

1 large onion, roughly chopped

4 garlic cloves, peeled and crushed

1 tsp dried oregano

1 tsp sweet paprika

200ml/7fl oz dry sherry

400g/14oz tin chopped tomatoes

2 tbsp tomato purée

salt and ground black pepper

long-grain rice, for serving

Shopping List

750g/1lb 10oz boneless chicken thighs, halved

55g/2oz pancetta, diced

115g/4oz chorizo sausage, sliced into 1cm/½in pieces

1 red pepper, seeded and cut into 2.5cm/1in cubes

fresh crusty bread, for serving (optional)

1. Preheat the oven to 180°C/350°F/Gas 4.

2. Heat 2 tbsp **olive oil** in a large flameproof casserole over a medium heat. Brown the **chicken**, in batches, on all sides for 4–5 minutes. Remove and set aside.

3. Add the **onion, garlic, pancetta** and **chorizo** and cook over a medium heat for 5 minutes, stirring from time to time. Then add the **oregano, paprika** and **red pepper** and cook for a further 5 minutes before adding the **sherry, tomatoes** and **tomato purée.** Bring to the boil, then return the chicken to the casserole, cover with a lid and pop into the oven for 45 minutes until the chicken is cooked through.

4. Season to taste and serve with **rice** and **fresh crusty bread.**

Antony's tip: buy thighs with or without skin, it's up to you. You can occasionally find good-value drumsticks and these will work just as well, but chop 2.5cm/1in off the thin end to allow the meat to shrink off the bone.

More ideas: a few green olives thrown in at the end would be traditional, but I'm not a fan.

This is a great way to make a chicken breast more interesting.

Parmesan-crusted chicken on a stew of white beans

1. In a food processor, blitz together the **half the Parma ham**, the **Parmesan, oregano** and **1 tbsp olive oil.** Add the **bread** and blitz until all the bread has become breadcrumbs. Tip onto a plate and season.

2. Place the **chicken fillets** between 2 layers of cling film and bash with a meat mallet or rolling pin until flattened.

3. Put the **beaten eggs** on a deep plate. Dip the chicken fillets first into the egg and then into the breadcrumb mixture. Heat a large frying pan over a medium heat with **3 tbsp olive oil** and cook the chicken fillets for 3 minutes on each side until golden and cooked through.

4. Meanwhile, heat another pan with the **remaining olive oil** and fry the **remaining Parma ham** and **chorizo** until crisp and cooked (about 4 minutes). Add the **white beans** and **mint.** Cook until hot, then season with **lemon juice** and **salt and black pepper**

5. Place the bean stew in the centre of 4 small warm plates, top with the chicken and serve immediately.

Antony's tip: chicken fillets are the small, arrow-shaped fillets attached to the breast. They are often sold separately in supermarkets.

More ideas: add a small tin of chopped tomatoes to the chorizo and ham, boil until the sauce thickens, then add the beans.

Store Cupboard

25g/1oz Parmesan, grated
1 tsp dried oregano
8 tbsp olive oil
55g/2oz white bread, crusts removed
salt and ground black pepper
2 large eggs, beaten
2 x 400g/14oz tins white beans, such as haricot or flageolet, rinsed and drained
juice of ½ lemon

Shopping List

115g/4oz Parma ham, diced
675g/1½lb small chicken fillets
115g/4oz chorizo sausage, diced
1 tbsp chopped mint

10 minutes
prep

35 minutes
cook

This classic curry is very rich so make sure you serve plenty of vegetables and rice with it ...

In the style of butter chicken

Store Cupboard

1 tbsp vegetable oil

85g/3oz unsalted butter

2 tsp garam masala

2 tsp sweet paprika

2 tsp ground coriander

5cm/2in root ginger, peeled and grated

½ tsp chilli powder

1 cinnamon stick

6 cardamom pods, crushed

350g/12oz passata

1 tbsp caster sugar

juice of 1 lemon

basmati rice, for serving

Shopping List

675g/1½lb boneless, skinless chicken thighs,

125g/4½ oz Greek yoghurt

150ml/¼pt double cream

naan breads, for serving

1. Heat a wok or large saucepan with the **vegetable oil** over a medium heat. Cut the **chicken thighs** into quarters. Brown them, in batches if necessary, remove and set aside.

2. Add **butter** and **all the spices** and fry for 1–2 minutes until fragrant. Return the chicken pieces to the pan, stir, then add the **passata** and **sugar** and simmer for 15 minutes until the sauce starts to thicken.

3. Stir in the **yoghurt, cream** and **lemon juice** and simmer for 5 minutes or until the chicken is cooked through, stirring from time to time. Serve with **rice** and **naan bread.**

More ideas: try this recipe with chicken breast or turkey and a handful of cherry tomatoes.

15 minutes
prep

10 minutes
cook

QUICK
& EASY

I used to eat veal schnitzel with lovely crispy breadcrumbs, often topped with a fried egg, but then Dutch veal became non-PC. I think chicken works very well in its place.

Breaded chicken escalopes with lemon and parsley butter

1. Place each **chicken breast** between 2 sheets of cling film and, with a meat mallet or rolling pin, flatten into large escalopes 1cm/½in thick.

2. Mix together the **mustard, honey** and **lemon zest.** Brush this mixture liberally on both sides of the escalopes. Put the **breadcrumbs** on a flat plate, then coat both sides of the chicken with them. Push the breadcrumbs firmly into the mustardy mixture, then pat them flat with a palate knife or fish slice.

3. Heat 2 tbsp **olive oil** in each of 2 large frying pans and cook the escalopes over a low heat for 3 minutes each side until golden and cooked through. Remove and keep warm, discarding any remaining oil in the pans.

4. Add **half the butter** to each pan and when foaming add the **lemon juice** and **parsley** and allow to sizzle. Spoon the parsley butter over the chicken and serve with **buttered spinach** and **lyonnaise potatoes.**

Antony's tip: if you want a thicker crust to the chicken escalopes, after pasting them with mustard, dip them in flour and then beaten egg before the breadcrumbs.

More ideas: pork escalopes make a good substitute for the chicken and 1 tbsp rinsed capers added to the butter along with the parsley and lemon provide a little zest.

Store Cupboard

2 tbsp English mustard

3 tbsp thick runny honey

grated zest and juice of
  1 lemon

150g/5½oz dried white
  breadcrumbs

olive oil

55g/2oz unsalted butter

Shopping List

4 boneless, skinless
  chicken breasts

2 tbsp finely chopped
  parsley

buttered spinach, for
  serving

lyonnaise potatoes, for
  serving (see p.185)

I love Japanese food, especially anything involving miso. Here I use chicken thighs because in a stew they remain more succulent than chicken breasts.

Miso chicken with emerald vegetables

Store Cupboard

3 tbsp runny honey

6 tbsp mirin or dry sherry

vegetable oil

2 garlic cloves, peeled and crushed

salt

long-grain rice, for serving

Shopping List

6 tbsp miso paste

6 boneless, skinless chicken thighs,

4 spring onions, cut into 2.5cm/1in pieces

115g/4oz extra fine beans, cut into 2.5cm/1in pieces

115g/4oz peas, fresh or frozen

handful of baby spinach, washed

1. Mix together the **miso paste, honey** and **mirin or sherry.** Cut the **chicken thighs** into 2.5cm/1in pieces and pop them in the miso mixture. Cover and marinate for 20 minutes at room temperature.

2. Put the **vegetable oil** in a large frying pan over a medium heat. Remove the chicken from the marinade and fry until golden and cooked through (about 15 minutes). After 10 minutes of cooking, add the **garlic** and **spring onions.** Toss to combine.

3. While the chicken is cooking, heat a small pan of salted water until boiling, then cook the **beans** and **peas** for 3 minutes.

4. Drain the vegetables, then add to the cooked chicken with the **spinach** and the remaining marinade. Toss to combine and cook, stirring occasionally, until the spinach has wilted and the marinade is sticky (about 3 minutes). Serve with plain **rice.**

Antony's tip: don't let exotic-sounding ingredients put you off; miso paste is now as widely available as mirin.

More ideas: use any green vegetable – I particularly like pak choi or purple sprouting broccoli.

Wagamama restaurants made eating "Oriental in a bowl" very popular in the UK. This dish is so easy and yet so nutritious and tasty.

Duck in a pot

1. Trim the excess fat from the **duck breasts** and score the skin (don't penetrate to the flesh) in a crisscross pattern with the tip of a sharp knife. Rub the flesh and skin with the **five-spice powder** and ½ **tsp salt.**

2. Heat a non-stick frying pan. Put in the duck, skin-side down, and cook over a gentle heat to crisp the skin and release the fat (about 10 minutes). Tip the liquid fat into a bowl from time to time. Flip the duck over and fry, flesh-side down, until cooked pink (about 3 minutes).

3. Meanwhile, boil a large saucepan of salted water. In another saucepan, bring the **chicken consommé** and **star anise** to the boil, then simmer for 5 minutes. Add the **spring onions, sugar snaps** and **pak choi** and simmer for 2 minutes.

4. At the same time, cook the **somen noodles** in the boiling salted water for 2 minutes or until al dente. Drain and divide between 4 warm bowls.

5. Ladle the broth and vegetables onto the noodles. Slice each duck breast into about 7 pieces and lay, skin-side up, on top of the noodles. Serve piping hot.

Antony's tip: cooking the duck breast mainly on the skin side helps to release fat and keep the duck tender.

More ideas: there's a whole host of different noodles, so don't worry if you can't get somen; just use another variety.

Store Cupboard
2 tsp five-spice powder
salt
3 whole star anise

Shopping List
4 duck breasts, skin on
3 x 415g/14½oz tins chicken consommé
4 spring onions, finely sliced
115g/4oz sugar snap peas
2 heads pak choi, roughly chopped
200g/7oz dried somen noodles

It makes sense to have a fish curry recipe, as you're unlikely to order one from your local takeaway. It's quick and easy as long as you've got a food processor ... every aspiring cook needs one.

Oriental fish curry

Store Cupboard

1 large onion, roughly chopped

3 garlic cloves, peeled

2.5cm/1in root ginger, peeled and grated

1/2 tsp ground cardamom

1 tbsp tomato purée

1 tbsp vegetable oil

400ml/14fl oz tin coconut milk

1 tbsp Thai fish sauce (nam pla)

juice of 1 lime

basmati or long-grain rice, for serving

Shopping List

1 tsp sambal oelek or 1 hot red chilli, finely chopped

1 stem lemongrass, outer skin removed, roughly chopped

1 medium bunch coriander, roughly chopped

115g/4oz French beans, topped, tailed and cut into 2.5cm/1 inch pieces

450g/1lb white fish fillets, skinned and cut into 2.5cm/1 in cubes

16 raw tiger prawns, peeled

1. In a food processor, put the **onion, garlic, sambal oelek or chilli, ginger, lemongrass, half the coriander, ground cardamom** and **tomato purée** and blitz to a smooth paste.

2. Place a wok or large saucepan over a medium heat and add the **vegetable oil.** Add the spice paste and gently cook, stirring regularly, for 3 minutes.

3. Stir in the **coconut milk** and 400ml/14fl oz **water**. Bring to the boil, then reduce the heat and simmer for 15 minutes.

4. Add the **French beans** and cook for 2 minutes, then add the **white fish** and **prawns** and cook for 2 minutes before adding the **remaining coriander, fish sauce** and **lime juice.** Cook for 1 minute. Serve immediately with cooked **rice.**

Antony's tip: after you've added the fish, stir very gently or you may break up the chunks of fish.

More ideas: monkfish, although expensive, is the perfect fish for a curry.

10 minutes prep

20 minutes cook

You can just roast a bit of fish and eat it, but to improve your cooking you must treat your kitchen like a playground. Experiment a little – you won't always get it right, but you'll have fun making mistakes and you'll build up your confidence.

Roast halibut with mozzarella and tomatoes

Store Cupboard

salt and ground black
  pepper
olive oil
3 garlic cloves, peeled and
  finely chopped
4 anchovy fillets in oil,
  chopped
85g/3oz unsalted butter
juice of 1 lemon

Shopping List

4 x 175g/6oz halibut fillets
2 beefsteak tomatoes, each
  sliced into 4
½ tsp thyme leaves,
  chopped
150g/5½oz ball cow's milk
  mozzarella, cut into 8
  slices
1 shallot, finely chopped
2 tbsp finely chopped
  parsley

1. Preheat the oven to 200°C/400°F/Gas 6. Season the **halibut fillets.**

2. Place the **tomato** on an oiled flat baking tray, dot the slices with the **thyme, half the garlic, half the shallot** and **2 chopped anchovies.** Drizzle with 1 tbsp **olive oil** and season with ground **black pepper.** Put into the oven and cook for 10 minutes.

3. Meanwhile, put a large ovenproof frying pan on a medium heat with a little **olive oil** and cook the halibut skin-side down until the skin is crispy (about 6 minutes).

4. Remove the tomatoes from the oven and arrange them alternately with the **mozzarella slices** on each halibut fillet, creating scales – 2 slices of each per fillet. Return to the oven for 6 minutes, then remove the halibut from the pan and keep warm.

5. Place the roasting frying pan (be careful – very hot handle) over a medium heat and add the **remaining shallot, garlic** and **anchovies** with the **butter.** Cook gently for 3 minutes, stirring occasionally, until the anchovies break down. Add the **lemon juice** and **parsley** and allow to sizzle, season and then spoon over the fish.

Antony's tip: all chefs want to use buffalo mozzarella, but it's too wet for cooked dishes where you want it to melt; great for a salad, but not for cooking.

More ideas: if you don't like anchovies, leave them out.

15 minutes
prep

35 minutes
cook

SLOW
& EASY

One of my old childhood favourites was called sole Florentine and had a béchamel-based sauce. This version is much quicker.

Cheesy sole with creamy spinach

1. Preheat the oven to 200°C/400°F/Gas 6. Place the **cream** and the **Parmesan chunk** in a saucepan with a little seasoning and bring to the boil. Reduce the heat and simmer for 15 minutes until reduced by half (the cheese will be half melted).

2. Now place the **sole** in a lightly buttered frying pan, season and pour over the **wine**. Simmer for 2 minutes, then remove the sole, cover with greaseproof paper and keep warm.

3. Pour the Parmesan cream into the wine, bring to the boil and reduce until it has reached a sauce consistency (this will take about 8 minutes and is ready when it is thick enough to coat the back of a spoon), by which time the Parmesan should have melted. Remove any unmelted Parmesan rinds.

4. Meanwhile, wash the **spinach.** Put the wet leaves in a large saucepan and cook over a medium heat until wilted, season, then drain well, pushing out as much liquid as possible with the back of a spoon.

5. Divide the spinach between 4 gratin dishes, dot with **butter**, then lay 4 sole fillets in each dish. Spoon over the sauce. Combine the **breadcrumbs** and **grated Parmesan** and sprinkle over the sauce, dot with a touch more **butter** and bake in the oven for 10–12 minutes until golden and bubbling.

Antony's tip: using Parmesan rinds to flavour the sauce is cost effective, but remove them before serving.

Store Cupboard
salt and ground black pepper
150ml/¼pt dry white wine
unsalted butter
handful of soft white breadcrumbs

Shopping List
300ml/½pt double cream
85g/3oz Parmesan, half in one chunk including rind, half grated
4 lemon or Dover sole, each cut into 4 fillets and folded in half
750g/1lb 10oz spinach, tough stalks removed

15 minutes prep
30 minutes marinate

10 minutes cook

Plain bog-standard fish fingers are always a fall-back for the children's supper, so make your own and know exactly what goes into them. These ramp up the flavour scale and use an abundant fish.

Fish fingers with a coconut twist

Store Cupboard

4 tbsp light soy sauce

2 garlic cloves, peeled and finely chopped

juice of 2 limes

100ml/3½fl oz Thai fish sauce (nam pla)

4 tbsp mirin or dry sherry

1 tbsp olive oil

40g/1½oz plain flour

85g/3oz cornflour

vegetable oil, for deep-frying

2 limes, cut into wedges, for serving

Shopping List

700g/1lb 9oz pollack fillets

2 hot chillies, finely chopped

2 tbsp finely chopped coriander

3 tbsp desiccated coconut

chilli dip (see p.217 – A fiery little number), for serving

1. Cut the **pollack** into fish finger sized strips. Place in a bowl and add **half the chilli**, the **soy sauce, half the coriander**, the **garlic, lime juice** and **half the fish sauce.** Toss to combine, cover and leave to marinate in the fridge for 30 minutes.

2. Meanwhile, put the **remaining chilli, coriander** and **fish sauce** with the **mirin or sherry, olive oil, flour, cornflour** and **coconut** into a food processor and blitz to a batter with the consistency of single cream. If necessary, thin the batter with a little water. Pour into a bowl.

3. Pour **vegetable oil** into a deep-fat fryer or a deep saucepan. (The oil should be at least 7.5cm/3in deep in a saucepan.) Heat to 180°C/350°F or until a cube of bread browns in 20 seconds. Remove the fish from the marinade. Dip it into the batter and straight into the oil – don't overcrowd the pan – and fry for 3 minutes until golden and cooked through. Remove, drain on kitchen paper and keep warm while you cook the remaining fish. Serve with a **chilli dip** and **lime wedges.**

More ideas : if you're not fond of coconut, no problem, just leave it out; for a crisper finish, dip the fish into the batter then into a mixture of two-thirds breadcrumbs to one-third desiccated coconut.

Come on, you've got to let me have one cod dish. If you buy Icelandic cod, you'll not have the food police on your back and it is delicious.

Roast cod with watercress and green peppercorn cream

1. Preheat the oven to 200°C/400°F/Gas 6. Heat an ovenproof frying pan with the **olive oil** and **butter.** Place the **cod** in the pan, skin-side down, and cook over a high heat, basting the cod, for 2 minutes. Then pop the pan into the oven for 12 minutes, basting from time to time.

2. Meanwhile, blend the **watercress, crème fraîche, flour** and **lemon juice** in a food processor until smooth, pour the mixture into a saucepan and heat gently until thickened (about 8 minutes). Add the **peppercorns, egg yolk** and **salt** and continue to heat gently until the sauce is thick enough to coat the back of a spoon. Do not boil.

3. Spoon the sauce onto 4 warm plates and top with the cod. Garnish with **watercress sprigs** and serve with **new potatoes.**

Antony's tip: for a smoother sauce, pass the purée through a sieve before adding the peppercorns and egg yolk.

Store Cupboard

1 tbsp olive oil

25g/1oz unsalted butter

2 tsp plain flour

juice of 1 lemon

1 large egg yolk

pinch of salt

Shopping List

4 x 175g/6oz cod fillets,
 skin on

100g bag of watercress
 (keep a few sprigs for the
 garnish)

300ml/½pt crème fraîche

2 tsp green peppercorns in
 brine, drained

boiled new potatoes,
 for serving

10 minutes
prep

10 minutes
cook

Crispy salmon skin, hints of curry, the creamy peas and roast tomatoes all combine to make this an appealing supper dish.

Fillet of salmon with creamy peas and curried tomatoes

Store Cupboard

1 tbsp hot curry powder

1 tbsp plain flour

1½ tbsp ground coriander

salt and ground black
  pepper

55g/2oz unsalted butter

2 tbsp olive oil

Shopping List

4 large tomatoes, halved

4 x 175g/6oz salmon fillets,
  skin on

150ml/¼pt double cream

3 spring onions, finely
  sliced

225g/8oz peas, fresh or
  frozen

2 tbsp finely chopped mint

1. Combine the **curry powder, flour** and **1 tbsp coriander** and season with ½ tsp **salt** and ½ tsp **ground black pepper.** Dip the cut surfaces of the **tomatoes** into this mixture.

2. Heat a large frying pan with **half the butter** and **half the olive oil.** Place the tomatoes, cut-side down, in the pan and cook over a medium heat for 6 minutes. Turn them over and cook for 3 minutes.

3. Meanwhile, heat another large frying pan with the **remaining butter** and **olive oil.** Dip the **salmon fillets** all over in the curried flour. Put them in the pan and cook, skin-side down, for 6 minutes, then turn over and cook for a further 1 minute. Turn off the heat and leave the salmon in the pan until ready to serve.

4. At the same time, heat the **cream** and **spring onions** until boiling, then simmer for 3 minutes before adding the **peas, mint** and the **remaining coriander.** Continue to simmer for 4 minutes, then season.

5. Spoon the pea mixture into the centre of 4 warm plates, place the salmon on top, skin-side up, and serve with 2 tomato halves.

Antony's tip: always flour fish skin if you like it crispy. Cook the fish for four-fifths of the cooking time on the skin side. Turn the fish over onto the flesh, turn off the heat and leave it in the pan for the remainder of the cooking time.

More ideas: use finely shredded Savoy cabbage instead of peas; try sea bass in place of the salmon.

10 minutes
prep

20 minutes
cook

QUICK
& EASY

When was the last time you saw scampi provençale on the menu, an old boys' classic that stretches back to the Seventies? I'm going to use frozen scampi since it's much easier; you don't want to be mucking about with langoustines, as great as they are. Give this a shot and relive the past.

Scampi provençale

1. Mix the **scampi** and **lemon juice.** Season and leave for 10 minutes.

2. Heat a large frying pan with the **olive oil.** Add the scampi and fry for 1 minute each side over a medium heat. Remove and set aside.

3. To the same frying pan add the **garlic, onion** and **butter.** Cook over a gentle heat for 8–10 minutes until the onion has softened but not coloured. Add the **oregano** and **wine** and boil, stirring occasionally, until most of the liquid has evaporated – there should be about 2 tbsp left. Then add the **tomatoes** and boil until thick.

4. Return the scampi to the pan with the **parsley.** Toss to combine, heat through and season. Serve with freshly cooked **rice.**

Antony's tip: don't overcook the scampi; you just want to tighten the scampi flesh.

More ideas: chunks of monkfish make a nice alternative to scampi.

Store Cupboard

juice of ½ lemon
salt and ground black
  pepper
2 tbsp olive oil
4 garlic cloves, peeled and
  crushed
1 onion, finely diced
25g/1oz unsalted butter
1 tsp dried oregano
100ml/3½fl oz white wine
400g/14oz tin chopped
  tomatoes
long-grain rice, for serving

Shopping List

32 scampi (not in
  breadcrumbs), defrosted
3 tbsp finely chopped
  parsley

10 minutes
prep

10 minutes
cook

QUICK
& EASY

I love to get involved with textures and crunch. These prawns, head on, shell on, provide tons. Serve with a nice dipping sauce, some new potatoes and a cucumber salad for a more substantial meal.

Salty griddled prawns

1. Drizzle the **prawns** with the **extra-virgin olive oil** and **lemon juice.**

2. In a bowl combine the **thyme, oregano, salt, pepper, garlic** and **garlic powder** and toss the prawns in this mixture, making sure they're well coated.

3. Place 2 ridged griddle pans (or cook in batches) over a medium heat and cook the prawns for 3 minutes each side until beige-pink and cooked through. Place them on 4 plates, scatter with **chopped parsley** and serve with **lime wedges** and an **oriental dipping sauce.**

Antony's tip: I use a pair of scissors to snip down the back of each prawn so I can lift out the black intestinal tract before cooking. Don't worry if you don't; the tract is tasteless and completely harmless.

Store Cupboard
2 tbsp extra-virgin olive oil
juice of ½ lemon
2 tbsp Maldon sea salt
1 tsp ground black pepper
2 garlic cloves, peeled and crushed
1 tsp garlic powder
2 limes, each cut into 4 wedges, for serving

Shopping List
24 large raw tiger prawns, shells and heads on
1 tsp finely chopped thyme
1 tsp finely chopped oregano
2 tbsp finely chopped parsley
oriental dipping sauce, for serving (see p.218)

Another 'sticky'; that gorgeous sweetness adds depth to the richness of the salmon and I love Chinese fried eggs, they're so crispy.

Teriyaki-style salmon, pak choi and Chinese fried egg

Store Cupboard

1 tbsp light soy sauce

2 tbsp mirin or dry sherry

2 tbsp rice vinegar

1 tbsp soft dark brown sugar

1cm/½in root ginger, peeled and grated

1 tsp sesame oil

salt

vegetable oil

4 large eggs

2 tbsp oyster sauce

Shopping List

4 x 175g/6oz salmon fillets, skin on

4 heads pak choi, halved lengthways

2 spring onions, finely sliced

1 hot red chilli, finely sliced

1. Stir the **soy, mirin or sherry, vinegar, sugar, ginger** and **sesame oil** together to make the teriyaki marinade. Add the **salmon**, cover and allow to marinate at room temperature for 15 minutes.

2. Place a saucepan of salted water on the heat to boil. In a wok put 5cm/2in **vegetable oil** on to heat, and heat a frying pan with 1 tbsp **vegetable oil.**

3. Cook the salmon, skin-side down, for 3 minutes in the frying pan over a medium heat, basting with the marinade from time to time. Cook for 2 minutes on each side, still basting, until the salmon is cooked through. Set aside and keep warm.

4. Cook the **pak choi** for 2 minutes in the boiling water. Drain and keep warm.

5. Crack the **eggs** into 4 cups. Make sure the oil in the wok is almost smoking, then working as quickly as possible, pour the eggs individually into the hot oil. Have a slotted spoon at the ready because they cook really quickly. After no more than 1½ minutes, remove and drain on kitchen paper.

6. Place the salmon with a little teriyaki glaze on 4 warm plates. Arrange the pak choi beside the salmon, then top the salmon with the fried egg. Drizzle each egg with the **oyster sauce** and scatter with the **spring onions** and **chilli.** Serve immediately.

More ideas: tuna steak instead of salmon works well, but keep it rare, cooking for no more than 1 minute on each side; Chinese fried eggs with a shake of oyster sauce make a good weekend breakfast.

15 minutes
prep

55 minutes
cook

In Spain one of my favourite tapas is crisp aubergine with chestnut honey. This dish sounds kind of weird too, but this is real playtime and the result works, for me anyway.

Stuffed aubergine with goat's cheese and jam

Store Cupboard

3 tbsp extra-virgin olive oil

juice and zest of 1 lemon

salt and cracked black pepper

up to 115g/4oz cherry or blackcurrant jam

Shopping List

2 aubergines, halved lengthways

280g/10oz soft goat's cheese

1 tsp finely chopped mint

2 tbsp double cream

crusty bread, for serving

1. Preheat the oven to 200°C/400°F/Gas 6. Heat a large ovenproof frying pan with the **olive oil.** Make shallow slashes in the cut surfaces of the **aubergines** and season. Place the aubergines, cut-side down, in the frying pan and brown over a medium heat (about 6–8 minutes), then turn them over and pop the frying pan in the oven for 30 minutes. Remove and leave to cool slightly.

2. Meanwhile, mash together the **goat's cheese, lemon juice and zest, mint, cracked black pepper** and **cream**, then season.

3. Scoop the flesh from the aubergines and roughly chop, combine with the cheese mixture and replace in the aubergine shells. Pop back into the oven for 15 minutes. Remove and spoon over the **cherry jam.**

4. Remove the stuffed aubergines from the oven and spoon over the **cherry jam.** Serve with **crusty bread.**

More ideas: substitute runny honey for the jam; the cheese mixture makes a good filling for beefsteak tomatoes and field mushrooms.

15 minutes prep   **1 hr 5 minutes** cook

This is perfect for vegetarians and meat eaters alike. The sweetness of the butternut contrasts nicely with the herby cheese.

Roast butternut squash with savoury ricotta

1. Preheat the oven to 200°C/400°F/Gas 6.

2. Arrange the **butternut squash**, cut-side up, on a roasting tray. Drizzle with **2 tbsp olive oil**, sprinkle with ½ **tbsp rosemary** and season. Place in the oven and cook for 50 minutes until roasted and caramelized.

3. Meanwhile, in a mini food processor, blend the **remaining rosemary, parsley, garlic, chilli flakes** and **nutmeg** to a paste then, with the machine running slowly, add the **remaining olive oil.** Pour into a bowl and mash together with the **ricotta, mozzarella** and **Gorgonzola**, then check the seasoning.

4. When the butternut squash is cooked, remove from the oven and fill the cavities with the cheese mash. Return it to the oven and cook for 15 minutes. Serve with a **green salad.**

More ideas: if Gorgonzola is not to your liking, replace it with 25g/1oz grated Parmesan.

Store Cupboard
6 tbsp extra-virgin olive oil
salt and ground black pepper
4 garlic cloves, peeled and roughly chopped
¼ tsp chilli flakes
pinch of grated nutmeg

Shopping List
2 small butternut squash, halved and seeded
2 tbsp rosemary leaves
1 bunch flat-leaf parsley, leaves only
175g/6oz ricotta
225g/8oz cow's mozzarella, diced
85g/3oz Gorgonzola
green salad, for serving

Vegetables

Spicy creamed spinach

Store Cupboard

55g/2oz unsalted butter

1 onion, finely chopped

1 tsp ground cardamom

2 garlic cloves, peeled and finely chopped

salt and ground black pepper

flaked almonds, for garnishing

Shopping List

750g/1½lb spinach, tough stalks removed
 and washed

150ml/¼ pint double cream

1. Blanch the **spinach** in boiling salted water until it wilts. Drain and push out all the liquid with the back of a spoon, then tip into a food processor and blend until smooth.

2. Meanwhile, melt the **butter** in a saucepan. Add the **onion** and cook over a medium heat until softened but not coloured.

3. Add the **cardamom** and **garlic** and cook for 2 minutes before adding the spinach and **cream**.

4. Heat gently, season to taste, then spoon into a serving dish and scatter with **flaked almonds**.

Aromatic courgettes

Store Cupboard

3 tbsp olive oil

2 garlic cloves, peeled and finely chopped

2 tbsp chopped, ready-to-eat dried apricots

2 tsp runny honey

2 tbsp sherry vinegar

Shopping List

450g/1lb baby courgettes, topped and tailed

12 mint leaves, roughly chopped

1 medium-hot red chilli, finely sliced

1 tbsp chopped macadamias

1. Heat the **olive oil** In a large frying pan over a medium heat. Add the **whole courgettes** and fry until golden, turning from time to time (about 5 minutes).

2. Add the **garlic** and **apricots** and fry for 3 minutes, stirring occasionally.

3. Add the **honey, mint** and **chilli** and toss to combine. Then add the **vinegar** and stir vigorously, scraping the bottom of the pan.

4. Scatter over the **macadamias.** Serve hot or at room temperature.

Indo-Franco beans with spices

Store Cupboard

2 tbsp vegetable oil

1 tsp yellow mustard seeds

1 tsp black mustard seeds

1 onion, finely chopped

2 garlic cloves, peeled and sliced

1 tsp cumin seeds

1 tsp ground coriander

1 tsp runny honey

salt and ground black pepper

Shopping List

350g/12oz French beans, topped and tailed

2 tsp chopped coriander

1. Heat the **oil** in a wok, add both colours of **mustard seeds** and stir-fry until the seeds start to pop.

2. Add the **onion**, **garlic**, **cumin seeds** and **ground coriander.**

3. Cook until the onion softens, then add the **beans** and 3 tbsp **water** and stir-fry until the beans are tender (about 5 minutes).

4. Drizzle with the **honey** and stir in the **chopped coriander**. Season and serve.

Tenderstem broccoli with chilli, garlic and anchovy

Store Cupboard

4 tbsp extra-virgin olive oil

4 garlic cloves, peeled and finely sliced

½ tsp chilli flakes

4 anchovy fillets in oil

salt and ground black pepper

Shopping List

1 hot red chilli, seeded and sliced

450g/1lb tenderstem broccoli, trimmed

1. Put the **olive oil, garlic, chilli, chilli flakes** and **anchovies** in a wok or frying pan over a high heat and stir until the anchovies start to break down and the garlic begins to brown.

2. Add the **broccoli** and 3 tbsp **water.**

3. Cook until tender, stirring from time to time. Season to taste.

Peas with lettuce and bacon

Store Cupboard

40g/1½oz unsalted butter

1 tsp caster sugar

salt and ground black pepper

Shopping List

4 spring onions, finely sliced

4 smoked streaky bacon rashers, rinds
 removed and diced

2 Little Gem lettuces, finely shredded

450g/1lb peas, fresh or frozen

150ml/¼pt double cream

2 tsp finely chopped mint

1. Put the **butter, spring onions** and **bacon**
in a saucepan and cook gently for 8 minutes.

2. Add the **lettuce, peas** and **cream** and bring to
the boil, then reduce the heat and simmer for
10 minutes.

3. Stir in the **mint** and **sugar** and cook for 1 minute.
Season to taste.

Oriental pak choi

Store Cupboard

salt

2 tsp vegetable oil

1 tsp sesame oil

1 tbsp soy sauce

1 tbsp oyster sauce

Shopping List

4 heads pak choi, leaves separated

1 hot red chilli, finely sliced

1. Bring a saucepan of salted water to the boil.
Drop in the **pak choi** and boil for 2 minutes. Drain.

2. Put the wilted pak choi in a bowl with the
vegetable oil, sesame oil, soy sauce and **oyster
sauce** and toss to combine. Sprinkle over the
sliced chilli.

Rosemary and garlic roast Med veg

Store Cupboard

100ml/3½fl oz extra-virgin olive oil

12 garlic cloves, peeled

2 red onions, each cut into 8 wedges

salt and ground black pepper

2 tbsp balsamic vinegar

1 tsp Dijon mustard

Shopping List

1 small bunch rosemary, stalks removed and
  roughly chopped

8 baby carrots, washed

4 courgettes, topped, tailed and halved
  crossways

8 asparagus spears, trimmed

4 baby aubergines, topped and halved
  lengthways

4 field (Portobello) mushrooms, quartered

1. Preheat the oven to 200°C/400°F/Gas 6. Place the **rosemary** in the bottom of a large roasting dish.

2. Put the **olive oil, garlic** and **vegetables** in a large bowl, season and mix well.

3. Tip the vegetables and oil onto the rosemary and roast in the oven for 30 minutes.

4. Mix together the **vinegar** and **mustard**. Pour over the roasted veg and toss to combine. Serve hot or at room temperature.

Twice-cooked parsnips and carrots

Store Cupboard

salt

2 shallots, finely chopped

1 thyme sprig

1 bay leaf

150ml/¼pt full-fat milk

1 large egg yolk

handful of soft white breadcrumbs

55g/2oz unsalted butter, plus extra for greasing

Shopping List

450g/1lb baby carrots, topped and washed

450g/1lb small parsnips, peeled and quartered
  lengthways

600ml/1pt double cream

1. Preheat the oven to 200°C/400°F/Gas 6. Butter a large gratin dish.

2. Blanch the **carrots** for 6 minutes in boiling salted water before adding the **parsnips** and cooking for a further 4 minutes

3. Drain the vegetables and return them to the pan with the **cream, shallots, thyme, bay leaf** and **milk**. Bring to the boil, reduce the heat and cook until the vegetables are tender (about 10 minutes).

4. Lift out the vegetables with a slotted spoon, leaving behind as much cream as possible. Stir the **egg yolk** into the cream.

5. Place the vegetables in the gratin dish, pour over the sauce, sprinkle on the **breadcrumbs** and dot with the **butter**. Cook in the oven for 20 minutes until golden and bubbling.

Thyme-roasted onions and potatoes

Store Cupboard

4 large onions, peeled

4 large floury potatoes, peeled

600ml/1pt vegetable stock

125ml/4fl oz extra-virgin olive oil

salt and ground black pepper

55g/2oz cold unsalted butter, diced

Shopping List

2 tbsp roughly chopped thyme

1. Preheat the oven to 200°C/400°F/Gas 6.

2. Cut 8mm/$\frac{1}{3}$in off the top and bottom of the **onions,** then cut them in half horizontally. Cut 1.5cm/$\frac{2}{3}$in off the top and bottom of the **potatoes,** then halve horizontally. Arrange alternately in a large roasting dish in one layer, pour over the **stock** and **olive oil,** then scatter over the **thyme** and season. Pop the vegetables into the oven for 40 minutes.

3. Take the dish out of the oven and carefully pour the liquid into a saucepan. Bring the liquid to the boil, then whisk in the **cold butter** a little at a time.

4. Pour this liquid over the onions and potatoes and roast for a further 25 minutes until the vegetables are nicely glazed.

A greener bubble and squeak

Store Cupboard

salt and ground black pepper

2 tbsp vegetable oil

Shopping List

175g/6oz mashed potato (either homemade or shop bought)

175g/6oz spring greens or green cabbage, cooked

6 spring onions, finely sliced

85g/3oz broad beans, fresh or frozen, cooked

85g/3oz peas, fresh or frozen, cooked

1 tbsp snipped chives

1. In a large bowl, combine **all the ingredients except the vegetable oil** and season.

2. Squidge the mixture into 4 patties and flatten them into burger shapes.

3. Heat the **vegetable oil** in a non-stick frying pan over a medium heat and cook the patties for 4 minutes each side until golden. Serve the patties immediately.

Beetroot and redcurrant mash

Store Cupboard

55g/2oz unsalted butter

1 red onion, finely chopped

6 tbsp port

1 tbsp redcurrant jelly

150ml/¼pt vegetable stock

1 tbsp red wine vinegar

salt and ground black pepper

Shopping List

4 medium raw beetroot

1 tsp thyme leaves

90ml/3fl oz double cream

1. Boil the **beetroot,** without topping and tailing, in salted water for 1¼–1½ hours until tender. Drain and leave to cool. Rub off the beetroot skins with your fingers (do wear rubber gloves – the juice stains) and roughly chop the beetroot.

2. Meanwhile, in a frying pan, heat the **butter, onion** and **thyme** and cook gently until soft (about 8 minutes), stirring occasionally. Add the **port, redcurrant jelly, stock** and **vinegar.**

3. Stir in the chopped beetroot and simmer the mixture for about 5 minutes until there is only a little liquid left. Pour the mixture into a food processor with the **cream** and blend until smooth. Season.

Curried mushrooms

Store Cupboard

1 tsp grated root ginger

2 onions, chopped

6 garlic cloves, peeled and chopped

100ml/3½fl oz vegetable oil

2 tsp ground coriander

1 tsp ground cumin

1 tsp ground turmeric

½ tsp chilli powder

1 tsp garam masala

salt and ground black pepper

Shopping List

4 tbsp Greek yoghurt

450g/1lb field (Portobello) mushrooms, sliced

2 tbsp roughly chopped coriander

2 tomatoes, seeded and diced

1. In a food processor, blitz the **ginger, onions, garlic** and **yoghurt** until smooth.

2. In a large saucepan, heat the **vegetable oil** and fry the **mushrooms** fiercely until they soften, but remove and set aside before they release their liquid. Add the **ground coriander, cumin, turmeric, chilli powder** and **garam masala.**

3. Stir for 2 minutes until aromatic, then add the yoghurt mixture and cook gently for 3 minutes. Return the mushrooms to the pan and cook for 10 minutes, adding a little water if it looks dry.

4. Fold in the **chopped coriander** and **tomatoes** and season to taste.

Potatoes in a salt crust

Store Cupboard

1kg/2lb 4oz coarse salt

2 tbsp plain flour

1 large egg white, lightly beaten

1 tsp peeled and finely chopped garlic

grated zest of 1 lemon

1kg/2lb 4 oz waxy salad potatoes, e.g. Anya,
  Charlotte or Ratte, peeled

Shopping List

2 tbsp finely chopped rosemary

1 tbsp soft thyme leaves

1. Preheat the oven to 180°C/350°F/Gas 4.

2. In a bowl, mix together the **salt, flour, egg white, rosemary, thyme, garlic** and **lemon zest.**

3. Spread a layer of this mixture in an ovenproof pan or terrine that is large enough to hold the potatoes. Lay the **potatoes** on top of it and then completely cover with the rest of the salt mixture.

4. Cook on a hob, over a high heat for 5 minutes, then pop the pan into the oven, uncovered, for 45 minutes.

5. Unmould the block of salt onto a tea towel, then gently crack it with a hammer to reveal the tender herby potatoes.

Perfect roast potatoes

Store Cupboard

1kg/2lb 4oz floury potatoes, e.g. Vales
  Sovereign, Maris Piper or King Edward, peeled

salt and ground black pepper

375g/13oz duck fat, pork dripping or olive oil

25g/1oz plain flour

12 garlic cloves, lightly crushed
  (optional)

Shopping List

1 tsp thyme leaves

1. Preheat the oven to 200°C/400°F/Gas 6. Cut the **potatoes** in half lengthways across their narrow sides so that each piece has one flat side and one rounded side.

2. Place the potatoes in a large saucepan, cover with cold water and add 1 tsp salt. Bring to the boil, then reduce the heat and simmer for 10 minutes. Drain into a colander. Place the

colander on the saucepan over a low heat to dry out for about 1 minute.

3. While the potatoes are simmering, heat a roasting tin of **duck fat, pork dripping or olive oil,** at least 1cm/½in deep, in the oven for about 5 minutes.

4. Mix together the **flour** with ½ tsp each of **salt and ground black pepper** and the **thyme** and sprinkle over the hot dry potatoes. Toss the potatoes quite vigorously, so that their edges start to break up.

5. Carefully place the potatoes, flat-side down, in the hot fat and baste the tops. Place in the oven for 20 minutes, then remove and turn the potatoes over with tongs. Return the potatoes to the oven and cook for a further 15 minutes.

6. Take the potatoes out of the oven and tip the majority of the fat into a heatproof bowl (duck fat can be reused – cover and keep in the fridge for a maximum of 1 month).

7. Add the **garlic**, if desired, to the potatoes and cook for a further 25 minutes for the crispiest roast potatoes – and lovely caramelized garlic.

Flavour-filled rösti

Store Cupboard

900g/2lb floury potatoes, e.g. Vales Sovereign,
  Maris Piper or King Edward, scrubbed

85g/3oz unsalted butter, for frying

1 onion, finely diced

2 tbsp melted unsalted butter

salt and ground black pepper

Shopping List

4 smoked streaky bacon rashers, rinds
  removed and diced

85g/3oz Gruyère, grated

1. Cook the whole, unpeeled **potatoes** for 10 minutes in boiling salted water. Drain and when the potatoes are cool enough to handle peel and coarsely grate (the centres will still be raw).

2. While the potatoes are cooking, heat **25g/1oz butter** in a frying pan and fry the **onion** and **bacon** over a medium heat until the onion is soft and the bacon is starting to crisp. Set aside and when cool tip them into a bowl with the grated potato. Add the **melted butter** and **Gruyère** and mix together. Season to taste.

3. In a large frying pan over a medium heat, add the **remaining butter** and when it has melted line the base of the pan with the potato mixture, neatening the sides and smoothing the top. Cook for 12–15 minutes. Cover the frying pan with a plate slightly bigger than the pan. Pressing the plate to the pan, turn them both upsidedown so that the rösti ends up on the plate, then slide it back into the pan and cook for a further 10 minutes until golden.

Baked potatoes with a surprise

Store Cupboard

4 large baking potatoes, scrubbed

150g/5½oz unsalted butter

1 onion, finely diced

salt and ground black pepper

4 large soft-poached eggs (see p.15)

Shopping List

4 smoked dry-cured streaky bacon rashers,
  diced

3 tbsp double cream

1 tbsp snipped chives

1. Preheat the oven to 200°C/400°F/Gas 6. Bake the **potatoes** for 1¼–1½ hours or until the skins are crispy and the flesh is soft.

2. Meanwhile, in a large frying pan over a medium heat, melt **25g/1oz butter** and fry the **onion** and **bacon** for about 8 minutes.

3. Cut one-third off the top of each potato, scoop out all the flesh from the top and bottom, being careful not to tear the skin, and discard the lid. Mash the flesh with a fork, folding in the **remaining butter, cream** and **chives**. Season well.

4. Spoon the onion–bacon mixture into the bottom of each potato shell. Top it with a **poached egg**, then fill the shell with the mashed potato, being careful not to burst the egg. The mashed potato will come above the rim of the potato. Pop back in the oven for 10–12 minutes until starting to brown.

Jansson's rosemary temptation

Store Cupboard

55g/2oz unsalted butter

12 anchovy fillets in oil, finely chopped

900g/2lb floury potatoes, e.g. Vales Sovereign, Maris Piper or King Edward, peeled and cut into 5mm/¼in slices

1 large onion, finely chopped

½ tsp ground white pepper

handful of soft white breadcrumbs

Shopping List

300ml/½pt double cream

2 tsp finely chopped rosemary

1. Preheat the oven to 200°C/400°F/Gas 6. Butter a large gratin dish using **half the butter.**

2. In a saucepan, heat the **cream, rosemary** and **any oil from the anchovies.** Bring the mixture to scalding point (just below boiling) then remove from the heat to allow the flavours to infuse for 10 minutes.

3. Arrange **one-third of the potatoes** in a layer covering the bottom of the dish. Scatter with **half the onion** and **half the anchovies.** Season with the **white pepper.** Repeat with another layer of each, finishing with a layer of neatly overlapping potatoes.

4. Pour over the cream, allowing time for it to seep between the layers. Scatter the surface with the **breadcrumbs,** dot with the **remaining butter** and bake for approximately 1 hour or until golden and bubbling.

Potatoes boulangère

Store Cupboard

unsalted butter

3 onions, thinly sliced

2 garlic cloves, peeled and crushed

675g/1½lb floury potatoes, e.g. Vales Sovereign, Maris Piper or King Edward, peeled and sliced 5mm/¼in thick

salt and ground black pepper

500ml/18fl oz chicken or vegetable stock

Shopping List

2 bouquet garni (or 4 thyme sprigs, 4 bay leaves and a few parsley stalks tied together)

1. Preheat the oven to 200°C/400°F/Gas 6. Melt 25g/1oz **butter** in a large frying pan over a medium heat. Add the **onions** and **garlic** and cook for 6 minutes, stirring from time to time, before adding the **potatoes** and cooking for a further 3 minutes. Shake the pan occasionally to combine the ingredients. Stir in 1 tsp **salt** and a few twists of **black pepper.**

2. Meanwhile, heat the stock to boiling point. Grease a 2-litre/3½pt baking dish with butter. Put in the potato–onion mixture, pushing it down and smoothing the top. Lay the **bouquet garni** on the top and pour over the **stock.** Dot with a little **butter,** cover with foil and pop into the oven for 1 hour. Remove the foil and return to the oven for a further 20 minutes to brown the top.

Twice-baked potatoes

Store Cupboard

4 large baking potatoes, scrubbed

1 tsp salt

½ tsp ground white pepper

175g/6oz unsalted butter, softened

¼ tsp grated nutmeg

3 large egg yolks

Shopping List

75ml/2½fl oz double cream

1 tbsp snipped chives

1. Preheat the oven to 200°C/400°F/Gas 6. Bake the **potatoes** on a rack over a roasting tray for about 1¼–1½ hours until the skins are crisp and the flesh is soft. Remove from the oven.

2. When the potatoes are cool enough to handle, cut a lid off the top of each potato (about one-third of the potato). Scoop out all the flesh from the body and lid, leaving the crisp shells intact. You can discard the lid.

3. Mash the potato until smooth, then fold in the **salt, white pepper, butter** and **nutmeg** and combine well. Fold in the **egg yolks, cream** and **chives.**

4. Spoon the potato mixture back into the potato shells, fluff up the tops and return to the oven for 20–25 minutes.

Perfect chips

900g/2lb floury potatoes, e.g. Mayan Gold,
  Maris Piper or King Edward, peeled,

vegetable oil or beef dripping, for deep- frying

salt

Buy yourself a deep-fat fryer – they are much safer and easier to use.

1. Cut the **potatoes** into chips the size you like:
straw – as fine as you can cut them
matchstick – slightly thicker
skinny – 5mm x 6cm (¼in x 2½in)
chunky – 1cm x 6cm (½in x 2½in)
jumbo – 2.5cm x 6cm (1 x 2½in)
massive – jumbo with skin on
game – thinly sliced crisps

STRAW, MATCHSTICK AND GAME CHIPS

2. Heat the **vegetable oil or dripping** to 190°C/375°F.

3. Cook the potatoes until crisp and golden (about 3–5 minutes). Drain well on kitchen paper, sprinkle with **salt** and serve immediately.

SKINNY AND CHUNKY CHIPS

2. Heat the **vegetable oil or dripping** to 160°C/325°F.

3. Blanch the potatoes in the oil until soft but not too coloured (4–7 minutes), then drain. (Allow to cool if you prefer to prepare ahead.)

4. Increase the temperature to 190°C/375°F and cook for a further 2–3 minutes until crisp and golden.

5. Drain well on kitchen paper, sprinkle with **salt** and serve immediately.

JUMBO AND MASSIVE CHIPS

2. Heat the **vegetable oil or dripping** to 140°C/275°F.

3. Blanch the potatoes in the oil until soft but not too coloured (8–10 minutes), then drain.

4. Increase the temperature to 190°C/375°F and cook for a further 2–3 minutes until crisp and golden.

5. Drain well on kitchen paper, sprinkle with **salt** and serve immediately.

Herby potato cake

Store Cupboard

4 large eggs, beaten

1 tbsp creamed horseradish

salt and ground white pepper

55g/2oz unsalted butter

Shopping List

2 tbsp crème fraîche

1 tbsp finely chopped chives

1 tbsp finely chopped dill

900g/2lb mashed potato (either homemade or
  shop bought)

1. Fold the **eggs, crème fraîche, chives, dill** and **horseradish** into the **mashed potato.** Season with **salt and ground white pepper.**

2. Melt the **butter** in a small frying pan over a medium heat. When it foams, put a quarter of the potato mixture into the pan and flatten it out as much as possible. Cook for 8 minutes.

3. Cover the frying pan with a plate slightly bigger than the pan. Turn the pan and plate upsidedown so that the potato cake falls onto the plate, then slide it back into the pan and cook for a further 5 minutes.

4. Keep the potato cake warm while you cook the remaining three. Alternatively, you can use a larger frying pan and cook one large cake, then cut it into wedges.

French mash (*pommes purée*)

Store Cupboard

675g/1½lb waxy salad potatoes, e.g. Ratte or
  Charlotte, scrubbed

salt and ground white pepper

200ml/7fl oz full-fat milk

200g/7oz cold unsalted butter, diced

1. Put the **potatoes** and ¾tsp **salt** into a saucepan. Cover with water, bring to the boil and the simmer until a sharp knife slips easily into the potato (about 20–25 minutes). Drain.

2. Peel the potatoes when they are cool enough to handle, then push them through a potato ricer, food mill or sieve back into the saucepan. Put the potatoes over low heat for no longer than 1 minute to dry them out a little, stirring from time to time.

3. Meanwhile, in another saucepan, bring the **milk** to the boil.

4. Turn the heat to low under the potatoes and incorporate the **cold butter**, bit by bit, beating it in vigorously with a whisk or wooden spoon, then pour the very hot milk in a thin stream into the saucepan, still stirring briskly. You should have a very smooth purée. Season with **salt and ground white pepper.**

Potatoes and mushrooms baked in parchment

Store Cupboard

1 onion, finely diced

2 garlic cloves, peeled and finely chopped

2 tbsp goose fat or beef dripping

675g/1½lb waxy salad potatoes, e.g. Charlotte, Anya or Pink Fir, scrubbed and cut in half if very large

salt and ground black pepper

Shopping List

4 smoked streaky bacon rashers, rinds removed and diced

225g/8oz button mushrooms, quartered

1 tsp soft thyme leaves

60ml/2fl oz dry Martini

1. Preheat the oven to 180°C/350°F/Gas 4.

2. In a frying pan over a medium heat, cook the **bacon, onion** and **garlic** in **goose fat or beef dripping** until soft but not too brown (about 8 minutes), stirring occasionally. Add the **potatoes, mushrooms** and **thyme,** toss to combine and cook for 3 minutes. Season to taste.

3. Place the contents of the pan in the middle of one large sheet of parchment paper or divide between 4 smaller sheets. Fold the parchment over the mixture so that the edges meet, then fold very tightly along the edges, forming a semi-circle as you go. Just before you finish sealing the parcel(s), pour in the **dry Martini.** Place on a baking tray and bake for 45 minutes.

Lyonnaise potatoes

Store Cupboard

900g/2lb waxy potatoes, e.g. Charlotte, Ratte or Pink Fir, peeled or scrubbed

½ tbsp salt

25g/1oz unsalted butter

1 tbsp olive oil

2 onions, thinly sliced

Maldon sea salt and ground black pepper

Shopping List

1 tbsp finely chopped parsley

1. Place the **potatoes** and **salt** in a saucepan. Cover with water and bring to the boil, then reduce the heat and simmer for 20 minutes. Drain. When the potatoes are cool enough to handle, slice them into 5mm/¼in rounds.

2. In a large frying pan, melt **three-quarters of the butter** with the **olive oil**, add the potatoes and pan-fry over a low heat for 15 minutes, turning from time to time.

3. Meanwhile, add the **remaining butter** to another frying pan and cook the onions over a low heat for 10–12 minutes. When cooked, fold them into the potatoes. Cook for another 5 minutes, then season with **salt and ground black pepper.** Sprinkle with the **parsley.**

Pudding

Mousses are always a family favourite. This one is light and fluffy and created by the use of gelatine.

Citrus mousse

1. In a chilled bowl, whisk the **egg whites** until soft peaks are formed. Add the **icing sugar** and beat for another minute.

2. In a small bowl, put 3 tbsp **boiling water** and the **powdered gelatine**. Leave to dissolve.

3. Put the **egg yolks**, **caster sugar** and **cornflour** in another bowl and whisk until they're well emulsified. Beat in the **orange juice, lemon juice**, **orange zest** and **orange liqueur**, if using, little by little, whisking constantly.

4. Pour the mixture into a saucepan and, stirring constantly, heat gently for 10–12 minutes without boiling. Add the gelatine and stir until completely dissolved.

5. Remove from the heat and fold in a tablespoonful of beaten egg whites to slacken the mixture, then fold in the remainder.

6. Pour the mixture into 1 bowl or 4 glasses and refrigerate for 3 hours. Serve well chilled, with **cream** or little **almond biscuits** if you like.

More ideas: replace the orange and lemon juice with the same amount of another sieved fruit purée (about 450ml/16fl oz) – strawberries, raspberries and blackberries spring to mind.

Store Cupboard

2 eggs, separated
1 tbsp icing sugar
2 tbsp caster sugar
1 tsp cornflour
juice of 1 lemon

Shopping List

1 sachet powdered gelatine
juice of 4 and grated zest
  of 1 orange
1 tbsp orange liqueur, e.g.
  Cointreau (optional)
fresh cream or almond
  biscuits, for serving

This was one of the few puddings my mother could make, so for that reason it has fond warming memories. It's a classic that I hope you'll enjoy as much as I do.

Saucy lemon pudding

Store Cupboard

100g/3½oz unsalted butter, softened, plus extra for greasing

175g/6oz caster sugar

4 large eggs, separated

40g/1½oz plain flour, sifted

400ml/14fl oz full-fat milk

juice and grated zest of 3 lemons

icing sugar, for serving

Shopping List

thick double cream, for serving

1. Preheat the oven to 180°C/350°F/Gas 4. With an electric hand whisk, beat the **butter** and **caster sugar** together until light and fluffy (about 5 minutes). Bit by bit, add the **egg yolks** to the creamed butter; the mixture will separate, but don't worry. Now add the **flour** and **milk** alternately, little by little, beating slowly with the electric whisk. Finally, stir in the **lemon juice and zest.**

2. In a very clean bowl with a clean electric whisk, whisk the **egg whites** to stiff but not dry peaks. Fold a tablespoonful of egg whites into the lemony mixture to loosen it, then carefully fold in the remainder.

3. Lightly butter a 1-litre/1¾pt baking dish. Spoon in the mixture, then stand the dish in a roasting tray. Pour hot water around it to come halfway up the sides. Bake for about 1 hour or until the top is golden and spongy.

4. Dust with **icing sugar** and serve with **thick double cream.**

More ideas: replace the lemon juice and zest with an equal volume of any fruit juice (about 6–8 tbsp) – try raspberry, orange, pineapple, strawberry …

I've been a trifle fan for as long as I can remember. This one is made in individual glasses so that the leftovers don't hang around in the fridge for days, but it is a real family-style trifle.

Trifle in a glass

1. Take 4 glasses and crumble about 2.5cm/1in **Madeira cake** into the bottom of each glass. Drizzle the cake with **elderflower cordial**, then spoon in a thin layer of **raspberry jam** on top of the sponge. Top the jam with a layer of **raspberries.** Keep back 8 raspberries to decorate the trifles. Pour on about 2.5cm/1in **custard**.

2. Whisk the **cream, sugar** and **vanilla** with an electric hand whisk until soft peaks form. Spoon it over the custard and then top each trifle with a couple of raspberries and a tiny mint sprig, if you like.

More ideas: the great thing about making individual trifles is that you can use elderflower cordial for the children and sherry for you and adult friends just by using a code to identify them – maybe 1 raspberry instead of 2; feel free to change the fruit and jam to suit your fancy.

Store Cupboard
55g/2oz caster sugar
1 tsp vanilla extract
4 tbsp raspberry jam

Shopping List
½ Madeira cake
50ml/2fl oz elderflower cordial
200g/7oz raspberries
300ml/½pt custard
300ml/½pt double cream
4 tiny mint sprigs (optional)

Make the most of British raspberries when they're in season. This pud takes no time at all and will impress family and friends.

Crunchy raspberry fool

Store Cupboard
115g/4oz caster sugar
juice and grated zest of
 1 lemon

Shopping List
350g/12oz fresh
 raspberries
350g/12oz mascarpone
150ml/¼pt double cream
4 meringue nests or
 85g/3oz meringues

1. In a food processor, blend **half the raspberries, 85g/3oz caster sugar** and the **lemon juice** until smooth. Strain through a fine sieve if you're worried about the pips, otherwise mix the purée with the **remaining raspberries** and **lemon zest**.

2. Tip the **mascarpone** and the **remaining caster sugar** into a large bowl and beat with a wooden spoon to loosen the cheese. In a separate bowl, beat the **cream** with an electric hand whisk to soft peaks, then fold it into the mascarpone mixture. Cover and refrigerate until ready to use.

3. Twenty minutes before serving the fool, break the **meringues** into bite-sized pieces, then fold into the mascarpone cream.

4. Take 4 large wine glasses and place a tablespoonful of the raspberry mixture in the bottom of each, followed by a layer of the mascarpone cream. Repeat. Finish with a layer of raspberry mixture. Serve chilled.

More ideas: substitute your favourite chocolate biscuit for the meringue; vary the fruit according to the time of year; 2 tbsp whisky or raspberry liqueur in the purée might help you sleep (for adults only).

Clafoutis sounds very impressive, but it's really just fruit in a batter. Don't get me wrong: it's delicious and once you've got the batter recipe the choice of fruit is yours.

Peach clafoutis

1. Preheat the oven to 180°C/350°F/Gas 4.

2. Break the **eggs** into a bowl. Add the **caster sugar** and whisk for 3 minutes to obtain a pale, light and fluffy mixture.

3. Fold in the **vanilla**, **flour**, **cream** and **milk** and mix well to form an emulsified batter.

4. Grease a 20cm/8in baking dish (4cm/1½in deep) with **butter**. Arrange the **peach halves** in the bottom of the dish, rounded side up, then pour the batter over and around the peaches. Bake in the oven for 45 minutes.

5. Before serving, sprinkle with the **icing sugar**. Serve with **custard, cream or ice-cream**.

More ideas: you can have fun playing with different fruit combos; try adding a few ground almonds to the batter.

Store Cupboard
2 eggs
115g/4oz caster sugar
1 tsp vanilla extract
45g/2oz plain flour, seived
unsalted butter, softened, for greasing
1 tsp icing sugar
85ml/3fl oz full-fat milk

Shopping List
125ml/4fl oz double cream
4 fresh peaches, halved and blanched for 2 minutes, or 8 tinned peach halves, drained
custard, cream or ice-cream, for serving

15 minutes
prep

1 hour
cook

SLOW
& EASY

A fab combo of two of my favourite fruits. Serve with custard or clotted cream – you're onto a winner.

Baked apples with rhubarb crumble

1. Preheat the oven to 180°C/350°F/Gas 4. Put the **rhubarb, orange juice and zest, half the sugar, cinnamon, nutmeg** and **orange liqueur** in a saucepan and bring gently to the boil. Reduce the heat and simmer for 6–7 minutes.

2. Cut the **Bramley apples** in half horizontally. Top each half with the rhubarb mixture, mounding it slightly. You will probably have a little left over.

3. Make the crumble by sifting the **flour** and **baking powder** into a bowl, then lightly rub the **butter** into the mixture with your hands, until it resembles coarse breadcrumbs. Fold in the **remaining sugar** and **almonds.** Sprinkle it over the rhubarb and apple, pushing down gently to form a crumble top.

4. Place the apple halves on a buttered baking tray and bake in the oven for 45 minutes until the apples are soft and the crumble is golden brown. Serve with **custard or clotted cream.**

More ideas: instead of rhubarb, use plum compote or peeled and diced plums, or a mixture of two-thirds peeled and diced eating apples with one-third blackberries.

Store Cupboard

175g/6oz demerara sugar
1 tsp ground cinnamon
1/2 tsp grated nutmeg
150g/5½oz plain flour
1 tsp baking powder
85g/3oz unsalted butter, plus extra for greasing

Shopping List

600g/1lb 5½oz rhubarb, cut into 2.5cm/1in pieces
juice and grated zest of 1 orange
1 tbsp orange liqueur, e.g. Cointreau
2 large Bramley apples, cored
85g/3oz chopped almonds
custard or clotted cream, for serving

20 minutes prep

40 minutes cook

Where have all the steamed puddings gone? My school used to produce one most days, but unfortunately none were as good as this.

Blackberry and apple steamed pudding

Store Cupboard

125g/4½oz unsalted butter, softened, plus extra for greasing

125g/4½oz caster sugar

125g/4½oz self-raising flour, sifted

2 large eggs, beaten

85ml/3fl oz full-fat milk

55g/2oz soft dark brown sugar

Shopping List

150g/5½oz diced Cox's apple, peeled

150g/5½oz blackberries

custard or thick cream, for serving

1. Preheat the oven to 190°C/375°F/Gas 5. Butter 4 individual heatproof pudding basins or ramekins.

2. With an electric hand whisk, beat the **butter** and **caster sugar** together until pale and fluffy (about 5 minutes). Add the **flour** and **eggs** alternately, little by little, until well combined. Fold in the **milk.**

3. Mix together the **apple, blackberries** and **brown sugar.** Divide this mixture between the pudding basins, then spoon the sponge mixture on top to fill the basins.

4. Cover each basin tightly with a sheet of foil pleated in the middle (to allow for expansion). Secure under the rim with string. Place the pudding basins in a roasting tray and fill with hot water to come halfway up the basins' sides. Cook in the oven for 40 minutes.

5. Remove the foil and run a knife around the rim of each pudding. Turn out onto warm plates, making sure the berries are on top. Serve with **custard or thick cream.**

More ideas: loads of toppings can be used – golden syrup, jam, marmalade, different fruit – just use a similar amount to the blackberries and apples.

20 minutes prep

1 hour cook

In a similar vein to tarte Tatin, but instead of puff pastry I'm using a sponge. This is a recipe inspired by a cake I saw in Harrods Food Halls, so it must be good!

Upside-down apple and banana cake

Store Cupboard

200g/7oz unsalted butter

85g/3oz soft dark brown sugar

200g/7oz caster sugar

1 tsp vanilla extract

2 large eggs

200g/7oz self-raising flour, sifted

Shopping List

5 Cox's apples, peeled, cored and each cut into 6 wedges

3 tbsp double cream

2 bananas, peeled and mashed

custard or double cream, for serving

1. Preheat the oven to 180°C/350°F/Gas 4. Melt **115g/4oz butter** in a 25cm x 5cm/10in x 2in ovenproof, non-stick frying pan with the **brown sugar** and **40g/1½oz caster sugar** and cook over a high heat for about 5 minutes until caramelized. Turn off the heat and then arrange the **apples**, cut-side up, in concentric circles over the caramel.

2. Meanwhile, make the sponge by combining the **cream, mashed banana** and **vanilla** with an electric hand whisk. Cream the **remaining butter** with the **remaining caster sugar** until pale and fluffy. Add the **eggs**, one at a time, beating vigorously, and then fold in the **flour** and mashed banana mixture alternately, a little at a time.

3. Spread the batter carefully over the apples, then put in the oven and bake for 50 minutes until golden and fully cooked. Leave to cool for 5 minutes. Cut around the sponge, then turn it out onto a plate so that the apples are at the top. Serve with **custard or cream.**

More ideas: most fruit can be used – peaches, banana, pears, apricots, plums – but avoid red fruits and berries, as they can be too liquid.

A great autumnal pud with our fantastic British pears – preferably use Williams.

Sticky ginger pears with mascarpone cream

1. Put the **sugar, half the honey, root ginger, wine, cinnamon, cardamom** and 150ml/¼pt **water** in a saucepan and bring to the boil. Reduce the heat and simmer until the syrup has reduced by nearly half (about 5 minutes), strain through a sieve and set aside.

2. Meanwhile, heat a large frying pan over a low heat. Add the **butter** and when it's foaming add the **pear halves**, cut-side down, and cook for 4–5 minutes until golden. Don't have the heat too high; you don't want the butter to burn. Turn the pears over and cook for a further 3 minutes. Add the syrup to the pears, cover with a lid and cook for 5 minutes to caramelize the pears, basting them regularly to build up a glaze. During the last 2 minutes of cooking, add the **crystallized ginger.**

3. While the pears are cooking, stir the **mascarpone** with the **remaining honey.** Place 2 pear halves on each plate, drizzle with the hot syrup and serve with a dollop of mascarpone.

Antony's tip: Conference pears may need to be cooked for longer.

More ideas: make the mascarpone cream less rich by replacing 115g/4oz mascarpone with 115g/4oz double cream.

Store Cupboard
55g/2oz soft dark brown sugar

5 tbsp runny honey

2.5cm/1in root ginger, peeled and grated

6 tbsp white wine

½ cinnamon stick

2 cardamom pods, crushed

55g/2oz unsalted butter

Shopping List
4 ripe pears, peeled, halved and cored

2 tsp finely chopped crystallized ginger

225g/8oz mascarpone

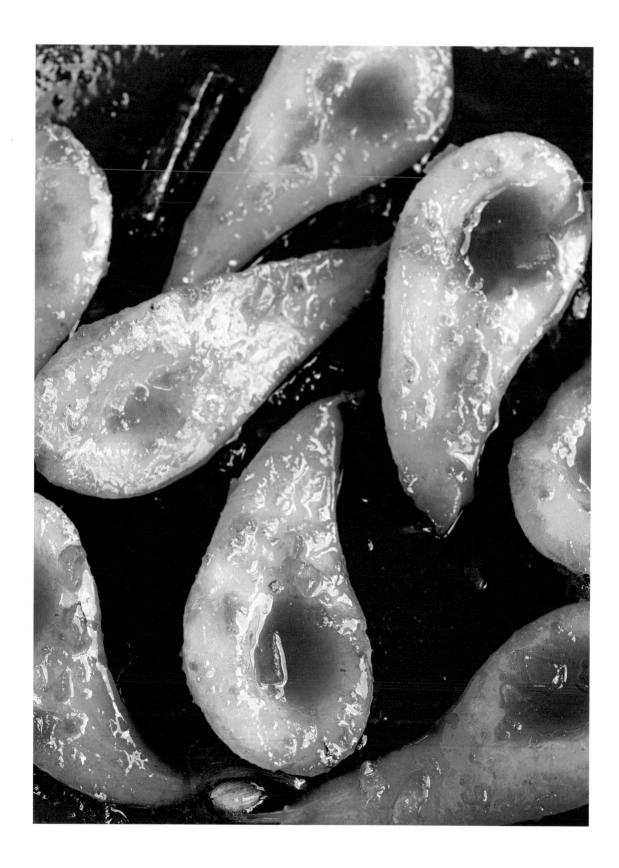

I'm pretty sure that this is my children's all-time favourite pudding, but I have to own up to never having made it for them. Maybe now they can make it for themselves.

That old favourite, banoffee pie

1. Melt the **butter** in a saucepan over a gentle heat. Set aside.

2. Crush the **biscuits** by blitzing them in a food processor or putting them in a plastic bag and bashing them with a rolling pin until they are fine crumbs. Stir the crumbs into the melted butter. Lightly oil a 27cm/11in loose-based deep tart tin and line the base with parchment paper. Pour the biscuit crumbs into the tin and press them down. Refrigerate for 30 minutes to set the butter.

3. Spread the **dulce de leche** over the biscuit base. Toss together the **bananas** and **lemon juice**, then arrange on top of the dulce de leche.

4. Whisk the c**ream** with the **coffee liqueur or syrup** using an electric hand whisk until soft peaks form. Spread over the bananas. Refrigerate for about 1 hour until set. Sprinkle with **chocolate shavings or toasted flaked almonds** before serving.

Antony's tip: dulce de leche is a very sweet toffee-flavoured paste that I've used here instead of the traditional condensed milk. It's becoming much more widely available in large supermarkets.

Store Cupboard
85g/3oz unsalted butter
vegetable oil, for greasing
juice of 1 lemon
2 tbsp chocolate shavings
  or toasted flaked
  almonds, to decorate

Shopping List
225g/8oz digestive biscuits
600g/1lb 5½oz dulce de
  leche (boiled condensed
  milk)
8 bananas, peeled and
  thinly sliced
600ml/1pt double cream
3 tbsp coffee liqueur e.g.
  Kahlúa, or coffee syrup

Not many puddings are as irresistible as bread and butter pud and it's a great way of using up leftover bread. This recipe is a variation on the classic theme.

Marmalade bread and butter pudding

1. Spread the slices of **bread** with the **butter** and **marmalade.** Cut off the crusts and cut each slice into 4 triangles.

2. Lightly butter a 20cm/8in square baking dish. Arrange 16 of the bread triangles in an overlapping layer in the dish, marmalade-side up. Sprinkle the bread with **a little of the cinnamon** and **some of the candied peel**, then repeat with 2 more layers, making sure the top layer is neatly arranged and finishing with a sprinkle of **candied peel.**

3. In a bowl, whisk the **eggs** until smooth, then add the **cream, milk, vanilla** and **sugar.** Whisk to combine. Pour this custard over the bread through a sieve to remove any unbeaten egg white. Let the pud sit for at least 1 hour to allow the bread to absorb the liquid.

4. Preheat the oven to 180°C/350°F/Gas 4. Place the pud in a roasting tray and pour hot water into the tray to come halfway up the baking dish. Bake in the oven for 1 hour until just set. If you want, sprinkle the top with a thin layer of **caster sugar** and either use a blowtorch to glaze or pop it under the grill until the sugar caramelizes.

Store Cupboard

12 slices day-old white bread

55g/2oz unsalted butter, softened, plus extra for greasing

4 tbsp marmalade, your favourite

1 tsp ground cinnamon

4 large eggs, beaten

225ml/8fl oz full-fat milk

1 tsp vanilla extract

175g/6oz caster sugar, plus extra for sprinkling (optional)

Shopping List

115g/4oz mixed candied peel

425ml/¾pt double cream

2 tbsp orange liqueur, e.g. Cointreau

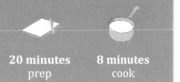

20 minutes
prep

8 minutes
cook

You'll go wild for this chocolate pud – it's so simple but so impressive. Make it once and it will become a regular feature at your table.

Warm chocolate nonsense

Store Cupboard

250g/9oz dark chocolate (55–70 per cent), broken into small pieces

55g/2oz unsalted butter

4 large eggs, separated

3 tbsp caster sugar

icing sugar, for decorating

Shopping List

90ml/3fl oz whipping cream

nibbed or crushed almonds, for decorating

crème fraîche, for serving

1. Preheat the oven to 140°C/275°F/Gas 1.

2. In a heatproof bowl set over a pan of barely simmering water (but not touching), melt the **chocolate** and **butter.** Stir to mix well and remove from the heat. Leave to cool a little, then gently fold in the **egg yolks,** one by one.

3. In a very clean glass bowl, whisk the **egg whites** with an electric hand whisk to soft peaks, then add the **caster sugar** and whip until stiff and glossy. In another bowl, whip the **cream** to ribbon stage (thick but not standing to attention). Fold the cream into the chocolate, then fold a tablespoonful of egg whites into it as well to loosen the mixture. Fold in the remainder of the egg whites.

4. Pour the chocolate mixture into 4 ovenproof gratin dishes, shallow rather than deep. Bake for 8 minutes until the mixture is warm and has developed a crust; you're not waiting for it to set. Sprinkle with **almonds** and **icing sugar** and serve immediately with a dollop of **crème fraîche.**

More ideas : pour the mixture over a couple of sliced bananas before baking.

25 minutes prep

20 minutes cook
3 hours chill

A classic French chocolate mousse with a creamy coffee topping; it's very rich, so you won't eat a lot.

Chocolate cappuccino mousse

Store Cupboard

150g/5½oz dark chocolate, (55–70 per cent), plus extra for grating

3 tbsp espresso-strength coffee

100g/3½ oz unsalted butter

3 large eggs, separated

2 tbsp caster sugar

Shopping List

150ml/¼pt double cream

3 tbsp Kahlúa or Tia Maria

1. Break the **chocolate** into small pieces and put with the **coffee** and **butter** in a heatproof bowl sitting over a pan of barely simmering water (the water must not touch the bowl). Leave to melt without stirring. Allow to cool for 10 minutes, then stir together.

2. Meanwhile, in a very clean bowl, whisk the **egg whites** with an electric hand whisk until stiff but not dry, then whisk in the **sugar** until stiff and glossy.

3. Add the **egg yolks**, one by one, to the chocolate mixture, beating well between each addition. Don't worry if the mixture looks as if it is splitting (separating); it will come back. Fold a tablespoonful of egg whites into the chocolate to loosen the mixture, then fold in the remainder, making sure there aren't any white spots.

4. Spoon the mousse into 4 espresso cups or wine glasses and refrigerate overnight or for a minimum of 3 hours.

5.Whisk the **cream** to soft peaks then fold in the **Kahlúa or Tia Maria.** Spoon on top of the set mousse and sprinkle with **grated chocolate.**

The combination of chocolate, vanilla ice-cream and banana is irresistible to most and this pud is a last-minute knock-together.

Anyone for a pud?

Store Cupboard
90ml/3fl oz full-fat milk

30g /1¼ oz caster sugar

200g/7oz dark chocolate
  (55–70 per cent)

25g/1oz unsalted butter

Shopping List
100ml/3½fl oz double
  cream

500ml/18fl oz tub best
  vanilla ice-cream

12 amaretti biscuits

3 bananas, peeled and
  thinly sliced

1. In a saucepan over a medium heat, cook the **cream, milk** and **sugar**, stirring from time to time until nearly boiling.

2. Meanwhile, break the **chocolate** into small pieces in a bowl. Pour over the hot cream mixture and stir to melt the chocolate, then whisk in the **butter** to give the sauce a good sheen.

3. Take the **ice-cream** out of the freezer for 10 minutes to defrost slightly, then spoon into a bowl. With your hands, coarsely crush the **amaretti biscuits** over the ice-cream and fold in the pieces. Scoop into 4 chilled glasses. Top with the **banana slices** and pour over the chocolate sauce.

More ideas: the tinned pears lurking in your store cupboard would go well with the almond and chocolate flavours.

Popcorn always goes down a treat when watching telly or a film. I'm offering you three different kinds, and all you have to do is follow the microwave instructions and then toss the popcorn with the toppings.

Popcorn nibbles

Cinnamon

1. Melt the **butter.** Toss the **cooked popcorn** in the butter. In a bowl, mix together the **sugar** and **cinnamon** and then sift it onto the buttery popcorn. Toss well to combine.

Store Cupboard

40g/1½oz unsalted butter

25g/1oz icing sugar

½ tsp ground cinnamon

Shopping List

microwave popcorn –
   1 quantity, cooked

Sticky butterscotch – the kids' favourite!

1. Put the **demerara sugar, soft brown sugar** and **butter** into a saucepan and bring to the boil. Cook, stirring from time to time, until the ingredients combine into a sauce (about 5 minutes). Leave to cool slightly, then pour onto the warm **cooked popcorn.** Toss well to combine.

Store Cupboard

55g/2oz demerara sugar

2 tbsp soft light brown sugar

55g/2oz unsalted butter

Shopping List

microwave popcorn –
   1 quantity, cooked

Garlic and chilli

1. Melt the **butter** with the **garlic, chilli flakes** and **salt**. Cook gently for 2–3 minutes to infuse the flavours, then add the **coriander or oregano.** Toss well with the warm **cooked popcorn.**

Store Cupboard

55g/2oz unsalted butter

2 garlic cloves, finely
   chopped

½ tsp chilli flakes

½ tsp salt

Shopping List

2 tsp finely chopped
   coriander or oregano

microwave popcorn –
   1 quantity, cooked

Useful Hot Sauces

White butter sauce

250g/9oz very cold unsalted butter; 2 shallots, finely chopped; 2½ tbsp dry white wine; 2½ tbsp white wine vinegar; salt and ground white pepper

Cut the **butter** into small cubes about 1cm/½in square and return to the fridge. Put the **shallots, wine** and **vinegar** in a small saucepan and bring to the boil, then reduce the heat and simmer for 5 minutes. The liquid should reduce by two-thirds. Cool for 5 minutes, then whisk in the cold butter, cube by cube. Keep the sauce warm, but do not let it boil. Season with **salt and ground white pepper.**

Antony's tip: if the sauce splits (separates), try rescuing it by whisking in 2–3 tbsp crème fraîche or double cream.

Béchamel sauce

60g/2¼oz unsalted butter; 60g/2¼oz plain flour; 1 litre/1¾pt full-fat milk; salt; ¼ tsp cayenne pepper

Make a roux by gently melting the **butter** in a saucepan until it foams. Dump in all the **flour** in one go and stir to remove any lumps. Stir continuously over a low heat for 2–3 minutes, then leave to cool. Meanwhile, in another saucepan, heat the **milk** to boiling point and then pour it over the roux. Whisk the mixture over a gentle heat until it's a lump-free sauce. Bring it to the boil, then reduce the heat and simmer for 10 minutes. Season with **salt** and **cayenne pepper.** Keep warm, covered with cling film, until ready to serve.

Antony's tip: I occasionally add a grating of nutmeg too.

Cheese sauce

Ingredients as for béchamel sauce plus
4 large egg yolks; 115g/4oz Gruyère, grated

When the béchamel sauce is almost boiling, whisk constantly and add the **egg yolks,** one by one. Stir in the **Gruyère** and cook until the cheese has melted, but do not allow the sauce to boil. Keep warm, covered with cling film, until ready to serve.

Bread sauce

2 bay leaves; 3 small onions, peeled; 2 cloves; 600ml/1pt full-fat milk; 2 pinches grated nutmeg; 25g/1oz unsalted butter; 100g/3½oz soft white breadcrumbs; 125ml/4fl oz double cream; salt and ground white pepper

Pin a **bay leaf** to **2 of the onions** using the **cloves.** Place them in a saucepan with the **milk** and **nutmeg** and bring to the boil, then reduce the heat and simmer for 15 minutes. Meanwhile, finely chop the **remaining onion.** Heat the **butter** in another saucepan and gently cook the chopped onion for 8–10 minutes without colouring. Strain the milk onto the sweated onion. Add the **breadcrumbs** and stir over a low heat until the sauce has thickened (about 15 minutes). Add the **cream** and season to taste. Keep warm until ready to serve.

A classic tomato pasta sauce

3 tbsp extra-virgin olive oil; 1 onion, finely chopped; 4 garlic cloves, peeled and finely chopped; 1 tsp dried oregano; ¼ tsp chilli flakes; 2 x 400g/14oz tins chopped tomatoes; 1 tsp caster sugar; salt and ground black pepper

Heat the **olive oil** in a saucepan over a medium heat. Add the **onion, garlic, oregano** and **chilli flakes.** Cook for 8 minutes, stirring occasionally, until the onion has softened. Add the **tomatoes,** bring to a simmer and cook very slowly for 35–45 minutes or until reduced and thick. Add the **sugar** and season.

Pepper sauce

25g/1oz unsalted butter; 1 tsp crushed black peppercorns; 2 tsp French mustard; 2 tsp Worcestershire sauce; 150ml/¼pt good-quality beef stock; 4 tbsp red wine; 2 tbsp green peppercorns in brine, rinsed and drained; 1 tbsp brandy; 150ml/¼pt double cream; salt

In a dry frying pan, heat the **butter** until foaming, then add the **crushed black peppercorns** and fry until aromatic. Add the **mustard, Worcestershire sauce, stock** and **wine.** Whisk to combine and simmer until the sauce has reduced by a third. Add the **green peppercorns, brandy** and **cream** and cook for a further 2 minutes. Season to taste with **salt.** Keep warm until ready to serve.

Onion gravy

8 onions, thinly sliced; 175ml/6fl oz red wine; 1 bay leaf; 600ml/1pt good-quality beef stock

Put the **sliced onions** and 2 tbsp **water** in a medium saucepan and cook very slowly, stirring from time to time, for about 1 hour until the onions are melting and caramelized. Add the **wine** and **bay leaf,** increase the heat and boil the wine until it has all but disappeared. Add the **stock** and simmer for another 20 minutes. Keep warm until ready to serve.

Antony's Tip: if you want a thicker gravy, add 1 tbsp plain flour to the onions and cook for 5 minutes before adding the wine.

A fiery little number

3 tbsp caster sugar; 120ml/4fl oz Thai fish sauce (nam pla); 4 garlic cloves, peeled and crushed to a paste with a little salt; 3 tbsp finely chopped mint; 1 tbsp finely chopped coriander; juice of 1 lime; 4 green bird's eye chillies, finely chopped

Gently heat the **sugar** and 3 tbsp **boiling water** and cook for 3 minutes until all the sugar has dissolved. Add the other ingredients, stir to combine and cook for 1 minute. Serve hot or cold.

Anchovy and basil sauce

4 anchovy fillets in oil; 2 garlic cloves, peeled; 6 tbsp extra-virgin olive oil; 1 tbsp balsamic vinegar; 3 plum tomatoes, peeled, seeded and roughly diced; 10 basil leaves, julienned; salt and ground black pepper

Mash the **anchovy fillets** with the **garlic cloves**. Mix in the **olive oil**, put in a saucepan and warm through gently. Add the **vinegar** and **tomatoes** and keep warm until ready to serve. Just before serving, add the **basil** and season to taste.

Butterscotch sauce

115g/4oz unsalted butter; 115g/4oz soft dark brown sugar; 4 tbsp golden syrup; 150ml/¼pt double cream; ½ tsp vanilla extract

Put the **butter, sugar** and **golden syrup** in a saucepan and bring to boiling point (you won't have to stir) over a medium heat. Add the **cream** and **vanilla** and stir to combine. Keep warm until ready to serve.

Hot chocolate sauce

115g/4oz dark chocolate (70 per cent), broken into pieces; 15g/½oz unsalted butter; 2 tbsp golden syrup; ½ tsp vanilla extract; 4 tbsp double cream

Put the **chocolate, butter** and **golden syrup** in a heatproof bowl sitting over (but not touching) a pan of barely simmering water. Leave everything to melt together, then stir to combine. Add the **vanilla** and **cream** and stir again. Keep warm until ready to serve.

Cold Sauces and Dips

A good barbecue sauce

2 tbsp vegetable oil; 1 onion, finely chopped; 4 garlic cloves, peeled and finely chopped; 2 tbsp fennel seeds; 2 hot red chillies, finely chopped; 600ml/1pt good-quality tomato ketchup; 100ml light soy sauce; 175g/6oz soft dark brown sugar

In a large heavy-based saucepan, warm the **vegetable oil** over a medium heat, then add the **onion, garlic, fennel seeds** and **chillies** and cook for 8–10 minutes until the onion is soft but not brown. Stir in the **ketchup** and **soy sauce** and simmer for 25 minutes. Fold in the **sugar** and cook gently for 5 minutes. Leave to cool.

Salsa verde

2 shallots, finely diced; 1 tbsp capers, rinsed and finely chopped; ½ tsp chilli flakes; ¼ cucumber, peeled, seeded and finely diced; handful of flat-leaf parsley leaves, finely chopped; ½ tsp anchovy paste (optional); 2 tbsp red wine vinegar; 175ml/6fl oz extra-virgin olive oil; salt and ground black pepper

Combine the **dry ingredients** in a bowl, then whisk in the **wet ingredients**. Season to taste.

Blue cheese

150ml/¼pt good-quality mayonnaise; 2 tsp white wine vinegar; 1 tsp Tabasco; 150ml/¼pt soured cream; 2 tbsp finely sliced spring onion; 85g/3oz blue cheese, crumbled, e.g. Roquefort, Barkham Blue or Stilton; 2 tsp snipped chives; salt and ground black pepper

In a food processor, blend together **all the ingredients except the chives and seasoning**, until smooth. Fold in the **chives** and season to taste.

Avocado mayonnaise

1 tsp horseradish sauce; ½ tsp Tabasco; 150ml/¼pt good-quality mayonnaise; 150ml/¼pt soured cream; 2 ripe avocados, halved, stoned and peeled; juice of ½ lemon; 2 spring onions, finely chopped; 1 tbsp snipped chives; salt and ground black pepper

Blend **all the ingredients** in a food processor until smooth, then season.

Oriental dipping sauce

1 tsp grated root ginger, peeled first; 1 garlic clove, peeled and crushed; 2 tbsp lime juice; 2 tbsp light soy sauce; 1 tsp sesame oil; 2 tsp runny honey; 1 tsp finely chopped coriander; 3 spring onions, finely sliced; 1 shallot, finely sliced; 1 red bird's eye chilli, finely diced

Mix **all the ingredients** together and leave for 30 minutes for the flavours to develop.

Tomato and horseradish sauce

150ml/¼pt sweet chilli sauce; 150ml/¼pt good-quality tomato ketchup; 1 tsp Worcestershire sauce; ½ tsp Tabasco; 1 tbsp lemon juice; 2 tbsp grated fresh or bottled horseradish; 1 celery stick, very finely diced

Combine **all the ingredients** and leave for 30 minutes for the flavour to develop.

Cocktail sauce

5 tbsp good-quality mayonnaise; 3 tbsp soured cream; 2 tbsp good-quality ketchup; 1 tsp tomato purée; 2 tsp Worcestershire sauce; ½ tsp Tabasco; 1 tbsp creamed horseradish; ¼ tbsp finely chopped dill (optional); ½ tbsp brandy; salt and ground black pepper

Mix **all the ingredients** together and season.

Sauce gribiche

2 large egg yolks; salt and ground black pepper; 175ml/6fl oz vegetable oil; 1 tbsp red wine vinegar; 1 tsp capers, rinsed and finely chopped; 1 gherkin, finely chopped; 2 large hard-boiled eggs (see p.15) peeled and finely chopped; 1 anchovy fillet in oil, finely chopped; 1 tsp finely chopped tarragon; 1 tbsp finely chopped parsley

Put the **egg yolks** in a bowl and season. Very slowly add the **vegetable oil,** a few drops at a time, whisking continuously, building up to a slow stream of oil. When all the oil is incorporated, add the **vinegar** and **remaining ingredients**. Check the seasoning.

Salad Dressings

Asian dressing

4 stalks lemongrass, outer skin removed and finely chopped; 6 tbsp rice vinegar; 2 tbsp caster sugar; ½ tsp finely chopped garlic; grated zest and juice of 2 limes; 2 tbsp finely chopped hot chilli; 4 tbsp Thai fish sauce (nam pla)

Place the **lemongrass, vinegar** and **sugar** in a saucepan and bring to the boil. Reduce the heat and simmer until the liquid has reduced by half (about 5 minutes). Strain the liquid, then add the **remaining ingredients** and mix well. Chill until ready to use.

French dressing

1 garlic clove, peeled; 1 tsp salt; 175ml/6fl oz extra-virgin olive oil; 60ml/2fl oz white wine vinegar; 1 tsp Dijon mustard; 1 tsp finely chopped parsley; 1 shallot, finely chopped; a few grinds of black pepper

Crush the **garlic clove** to a paste with a little of the **salt** then whisk **all the ingredients** together.

Creamy lemon dressing

3 tbsp extra-virgin olive oil; 1 tbsp vegetable oil; juice of 1 lemon; 2 tbsp crème fraîche; ½ tsp salt and a few grinds of black pepper

Whisk **all the ingredients** together until creamy.

Walnut and mint dressing

1 tbsp runny honey; ¼ tsp ground cinnamon; 2 tbsp extra-virgin olive oil; 3 tbsp lime juice; 3 tbsp walnut oil; 2 tbsp finely chopped mint leaves; salt and ground black pepper

Whisk **all the ingredients** together and season to taste.

Truffle dressing

2 tbsp extra-virgin olive oil; 1½ tsp white truffle oil; 1 tbsp lemon juice; salt and ground black pepper

Whisk **all the ingredients** together and season to taste.

Apple and ginger dressing

1 tbsp cider vinegar; 1 tsp runny honey; 1 Cox's apple, peeled, cored and diced; 2.5cm/1in root ginger, peeled and grated; 200ml/7fl oz dry apple juice

Place **all the ingredients** in a saucepan over a medium heat and simmer until the apple is tender. Pour the ingredients into a food processor and blitz until smooth. Pass through a fine sieve and leave to cool.

Herb salad dressing

2 garlic cloves, peeled and finely chopped; 2 tsp ginger juice; 3 tbsp chopped mint; 3 tbsp chopped basil; 2 tbsp chopped coriander; 3 tbsp groundnut oil; 3 tbsp lime juice; 2 tbsp runny honey; 1 tbsp Thai fish sauce (nam pla); 1 tsp chilli sauce

Combine **all the ingredients** and refrigerate until ready to serve.

Blue cheese dressing

150ml/¼pt soured cream; 150ml/¼pt mayonnaise; 2 tsp lemon juice; 2 tbsp chopped spring onions; 1 garlic clove, peeld and finely chopped; 1 tsp tabasco sauce; 115g/4oz Roquefort, crumbled; 3 tbsp freshly grated Parmesan; 3 tbsp Worcestershire sauce

Blend **all the ingredients** together in a food processor until thick and smooth. Don't worry if there are a few lumps of cheese. Place in an airtight container and refrigerate until ready to use.

Store Cupboard

Spices

Cajun seasoning
Cardamom pods
Chilli flakes
Cinnamon sticks
Garlic powder
Green peppercorns
Ground spices – 5-spice,
 cardamom, coriander,
 cumin, curry powder, garam
 masala, sweet paprika,
 turmeric
Juniper berries
Mustard seeds - black, yellow
Nutmeg – grated, whole
Palm sugar
Pepper – ground black,
 ground white
Saffron stamens
Salt – sea salt, table
Star anise

Herbs

Bay leaves
Dried herbs – rosemary,
 thyme, oregano
Lime leaves

Sauces

Apple sauce
Chilli sauce – hot, sweet
Dry sherry
Harissa
Hoisin sauce
Horseradish sauce
Ketjap manis
Mango chutney
Mayonnaise

Mirin
Mustard – Dijon, English,
 wholegrain
Oyster sauce
Port
Soy sauce – light, dark
Tabasco
Thai fish sauce (nam pla)
Thai red curry paste
Tomato Ketchup
Wine – red, white

Vinegars and Oils

Oil – olive, sesame,
 vegetable, walnut
Vinegar – balsamic, rice,
 sherry, white wine

Tins and Jars

Capers, in salt or brine
Coconut milk
Jam/marmalade
Redcurrant jelly
Tinned beans – cannellini,
 chickpeas, flageolet,
 white beans
Tinned fish – anchovy fillets,
 crabmeat, tuna
Tomatoes – chopped,
 sun-dried, passata, whole,
Pesto – green, red

Baking

Almonds – flaked, ground,
 toasted
Baking powder
Cornflour

Dark chocolate (55–70 per cent)
Eggs
Flour – plain, self-raising
Golden syrup
Honey – runny, set
Sugar – caster, demerara,
 icing, soft dark brown
Vanilla extract

Staple Vegetables

Garlic
Lemons
Onions – red, white
Potatoes – floury, new,
 waxy
Root ginger

Dry Stores

Dried fruits - apricots, prunes
Espresso coffee
Lentils – green, Puy
Noodles – egg, rice
Pasta – penne, spaghetti
Rice – basmati, brown,
 long-grain
Stock cubes – chicken,
 vegetable
White bread
White breadcrumbs

Fridge/Freezer

Cheese – Cheddar, Parmesan
Frozen peas
Ice cubes
Milk
Unsalted butter

Index

almonds 30, 94
amaretti biscuits 212
anchovies
    anchovy and basil sauce 217
    anchovy soldiers 25
    as ingredient 37, 51, 121, 142, 165
apples
    apple and ginger dressing 219
    baked, with rhubarb crumble 197
    blackberry and apple steamed pudding 198
    in fruity breakfast compôte 41
    in salad 94
    upside-down apple and banana cake 200
apricots, in fruity breakfast compôte 41
Asian [salad] dressing 219
asparagus 169
aubergines
    in Moroccan salad 89
    stuffed, with goat's cheese and jam 156
    as ingredient 169
avocado, with prawns 77
avocado mayonnaise 218

bacon
    with baked potatoes 50, 177
    with chicken in a bag 109
    with liver, sage and lyonnaise potatoes 120
    with peas and lettuce 166
    with pot-roast pheasant 126
    prawn, bacon and garlic pitta pockets 64
    with roast field mushrooms, anchovy and tomato 51
    in a rösti 177
    in tartiflette 48
    as ingredient 18, 22, 24, 26, 30, 37, 56, 92, 104, 185
    see also pancetta
bagels, smoked salmon 34
bananas
    banana and raspberry smoothie 42
    banoffee pie 205
    with ice-cream and chocolate sauce 212
    upside-down apple and banana cake 200
banoffee pie 205
basil, anchovy and basil sauce 217
beans
    broad beans, in bubble and squeak 170
    flageolet and haricot 109, 133
    Indo-Franco (French beans) with spices 165
    as ingredient 90, 136, 140
beef
    burgers with attitude 67
    chilli beef 125
beetroot
    with peppered smoked mackerel and horseradish 73
    and redcurrant mash 173
black pudding, in salad 92

blackberries, blackberry and apple steamed pudding 198
blackcurrant jam, stuffed aubergine with goat's cheese 156
bread
    bread sauce 216
    breakfast bread 30
    ciabatta *see* bruschetta
    tomato bread, chargrilled 33
bread and butter pudding, with marmalade 207
breakfast and brunch recipes 12–45
Brie, deep fried almond-coated Brie, apple and pear salad 94
broccoli
    tenderstem, with chilli, garlic and anchovy 165
    as ingredient 62, 121
brunch *see* breakfast and brunch recipes
bruschetta, with warm smoked duck with cherry tomato and rocket bruschetta 69
bubble and squeak 170
burgers, with attitude 67
butter
    lemon and parsley 135
    white butter sauce 216
butternut squash
    with pork escalopes 107
    roast, with savoury ricotta 157
butterscotch popcorn 213–15
butterscotch sauce 217

cabbage
    in bubble and squeak 170
    as ingredient 56, 67, 126
carrots 84, 169
casseroles *see* soups, broths, stews and casseroles
cauliflower, and courgette fritters with Gorgonzola dip 99
cheese
    blue cheese dip 218
    blue cheese [salad] dressing 219
    cheese sauce 216
    cream cheese 34, 50, 76
    goat's cheese with stuffed aubergine 156
    mixed Italian 28
    spread 29
    see also mozzarella; Gorgonzola; Gruyère; mascarpone; Parmesan; ricotta
cherry jam, stuffed aubergine with goat's cheese 156
chick peas 18
chicken
    in a bowl of nice rice 67
    breaded escalopes with lemon and parsley butter 135
    butter chicken 134
    Mediterranean chicken casserole 130
    miso chicken with emerald vegetables 136
    Parmesan-crusted on stew of white beans 133
    spiced chicken rolls 68

    sticky chicken nuggets 129
    supper in a bag 109
    in 'the ultimate pot noodle' 62
chicory leaves, with flatbread and dips 85
chillies
    chilli beef 125
    chilli dip 146
    chilli and garlic popcorn 213-15
    chilli sauce (a fiery number) 217
    with tenderstem broccoli 165
chocolate
    chocolate capuccino mousse 210
    chocolate sauce 212
    hot chocolate sauce 217
    warm chocolate nonsense 208
chorizo
    with baked eggs and red peppers 18
    with chicken in a bag 109
    in Mediterranean chicken casserole 130
    with Parmesan-crusted chicken 133
    with penne and squid 55
cinnamon popcorn 213-15
citrus mousse 189
clafoutis, peach clafoutis 195
coconut (dessicated), in fish fingers 146
cod, roast, with watercress and green peppercorn cream 149
compôte, fruity breakfast compôte 41
courgettes
    aromatic 162
    and cauliflower fritters with Gorgonzola dip 99
    with fresh and green spaghetti 95
    with leg of lamb steaks 117
    in Moroccan salad 89
    as ingredient 169
crab, crab and noodle omelette 82
cream 26, 29, 53, 100, 134, 143, 150, 169, 173, 178, 191, 192, 200, 210, 212
crumbles, apple and rhubarb 197
cucumber
    with flatbread and dips 85
    with marinated lamb 118
    with pork chops (Chinese style) 106
curries
    butter chicken 134
    curried mushrooms 173
    lamb curry (rogan josh) 113
    Oriental fish curry 140
    salmon with creamy peas and curried tomatoes 150

desserts see puddings
dinner 102–59
dips *see* sauces, relishes and dips
drop scones *see* griddle cakes
duck
    in a pot 139
    warm smoked, with cherry tomato and rocket bruschetta 69

eggs
    baked with chorizo and red peppers 18
    with baked potatoes 177
    boiled 15, 25

breakfast bread 30
Chinese fried egg 154
in chocolate capuccino mousse 210
fried 16, 154
in herby potato cake 182
omelettes 24, 82
poached 15, 22, 177
posh eggs 21
ricotta griddle cakes 38
sauce gribiche 218
in saucy lemon pudding 190
scrambled 16, 21, 83
in twice-baked potatoes 181
in warm chocolate nonsense 208
see also quiche

feta
with marinated lamb 118
with spring vegetable salad 90
fish
fish fingers with a coconut twist 146
Oriental fish curry 140
smoked fish paté 76
see also names of individual fish and
shellfish
flatbreads, and dips 85
fritters, cauliflower and courgette 99

garlic and chilli popcorn 213–15
garlic purée 64
ginger/ginger syrup
apple and ginger dressing 219
in fruity breakfast compôte 41
sticky chicken nuggets 129
sticky ginger pears with mascarpone
cream 201
gnocchi nuggets, with creamy peas and
prosciutto 53
Gorgonzola
in cheese spread 29
dip 99
in roast butternut squash 157
griddle cakes, ricotta with honey 38
Gruyère
with cauliflower and courgette fritters 99
in cheese spread 29
in a rösti 177
in tartiflette 48

**halibut, roast, with mozzarella and
tomatoes 142**
ham, Parma ham with Parmesan-crusted
chicken 133
herb salad dressing 219
horseradish cream 100, 182
horseradish sauce
baked potato filling 50
with peppered smoked mackerel and
beetroot 73
in posh eggs 21
smoked fish paté 76
with tomato ketchup 218
hot dogs 32

**ice-cream, with banana and chocolate
sauce 212**

lamb
lamb pilaf 110
leg of lamb steaks (Mediterranean style)
117

marinated on a Greek salad 118
meatballs with tomato and penne 60
rogan josh style curry 113
rustic roast shoulder of 121
stir-fried 112
tortilla wrap with Morroccan lamb 59
leeks, in winter warming soup 98
lemons/lemon juice
citrus mousse 189
creamy lemon dressing 219
saucy lemon pudding 190
strawberry, lemon and mint smoothie
43
lentils, a thrifty supper 104
lettuce
little gem 77, 166
with peas and bacon 166
liver, bacon and sage, with lyonnaise
potatoes 120
lunch 46–101

mackerel *see* **smoked mackerel**
Madeira cake, trifle in a glass 191
mangoes
curried mango dip 85
tropical mango smoothie 42
marinades
for Greek lamb salad 118
for miso chicken 136
for salmon sashimi 74
for squid salad 78
for sticky chicken nuggets 129
see also sauces, relishes and dips
marmalade bread and butter pudding 207
mascarpone
in cheese spread 29
in crunchy raspberry fool 192
sticky ginger pears with mascarpone
cream 201
meringues, in crunchy raspberry fool 192
Moroccan salad 89
mousse
chocolate capuccino mousse 210
citrus mousse 189
mozzarella
baked potato filling 50
in cheesy pancakes 28
in roast butternut squash 157
with roast halibut 142
muffins, English muffins in 'posh eggs' 21
mushrooms
baked in parchment with potatoes 185
curried 173
roast field mushrooms with bacon,
anchovy and tomato 51
in the ultimate pot noodle 62
as ingredient 22, 24, 56, 104, 169
mussels with a kick 80

noodles
crab and noodle omelette 82
somen noodles (duck in a pot) 139
the ultimate pot noodle 62

olives, with marinated lamb 118
omelette
breakfast omelette 24
crab and noodle 82
onions
onion gravy 217
in potatoes boulangère 178

thyme-roasted, with potatoes 170
in winter warming soup 98
orange, in citrus mousse 189

pak choi
in duck in a pot 139
Oriental pak choi 166
with teriyaki-style salmon 154
pancakes, cheesy 28
pancetta
in a hot dog 32
in Mediterranean chicken casserole 130
see also bacon
Parmesan
in cheesy pancakes 28
cheesy sole with creamy spinach 143
Parmesan-crusted chicken on stew of
white beans 133
in prawn, bacon and garlic pitta pockets
64
parsnips, twice-cooked, and carrots 169
pasta
fettucine/tagliatelle with spinach and
plum tomatoes 97
fresh and green spaghetti 95
meatballs with tomato and penne 60
penne with squid and chorizo 55
tortellini (ready-made), how to excite 56
peach clafoutis 195
pears
in salad 94
sticky ginger pears with mascarpone
cream 201
peas
in bubble and squeak 170
with fresh and green spaghetti 95
pea and spinach soup 100
as ingredient 53, 90, 136, 139, 150, 166
pepper sauce 217
peppers, red
with baked eggs and chorizo 18
in Mediterranean chicken casserole 130
with spiced scrambled eggs and
shrimps 83
pheasant, with cider and bacon (pot-roast)
126
pineapple passion, smoothie 43
pitta bread
burgers with attitude 67
and dips 85
prawn, bacon and garlic pitta pockets
64
pollack, in fish fingers 146
popcorn nibbles 213–15
pork
escalopes with spicy butternut 107
pork chops with Chinese flavours 106
pot noodles, the ultimate 62
pot-roast
pheasant with cider and bacon 126
rustic roast lamb shoulder 121
potatoes
baked in parchment with mushrooms
185
baked, with a surprise 177
baked (this year's model) 50
boulangère potatoes 178
in bubble and squeak 170
French mash (pommes purées) 182
herby potato cake 182
Jansson's rosemary temptation 178

with leg of lamb steaks 117
lyonnaise potatoes 120, 185
in Mediterranean chicken casserole 130
new potatoes with pork chops 106
perfect chips 181
perfect roast 174
with roast lamb 121
rösti 177
in a salt crust 174
in tartiflette 48
thyme-roasted, with onions 170
twice-baked 181
winter warming soup 98
prawns and shrimps
with avocado 77
in a bowl of nice rice 67
in fish curry 140
prawn, bacon and garlic pitta pockets 64
salty griddled prawns 153
scampi provençale 151
shrimps with roast peppers and spiced scrambled eggs 83
in the ultimate pot noodle 62
prosciutto, with gnocchi nuggets and creamy peas 53
pudding 186–215

quiche
naked mini breakfast 26
see also eggs

rabbit, rabbit legs with roast shallots and mustard sauce 128
radishes, with flatbread and dips 85
raspberries
crunchy raspberry fool 192
raspberry and banana smoothie 42
in trifle in a glass 191
redcurrant jelly, and beetroot mash 173
relishes see sauces, relishes and dips
rhubarb
in fruity breakfast compôte 41
rhubarb crumble with baked apples 197
rice
with butter chicken 134
lamb curry (rogan josh) 113
lamb pilaf 110
lamb stir-fry 112
with Mediterranean chicken casserole 130
with miso chicken 136
with mussels 80
nice rice (nasi goreng) 67
scampi provençale 151
sushi 74
ricotta
in cheesy pancakes 28
griddle cakes 38
with roast butternut squash 157
roasting bags, supper in a bag 109
rosemary
and garlic roast Med veg 169
Jansson's rosemary temptation 178
rösti, flavour-filled 177

salad dressings 219
salads
Asian squid salad 78

deep fried almond-coated Brie, apple and pear 94
favourite flavours 92
Greek with marinated lamb 118
Moroccan 89
spring vegetable and feta 90
Vietnamese crunchy vegetable 84
salmon
fillet, with creamy peas and curried tomatoes 150
sashimi with flavour 74
teriyaki-style, with pak choi and Chinese fried egg 154
see also smoked salmon
salsa verde 218
sashimi, salmon sashimi with flavour 74
sauces, relishes and dips
anchovy and basil sauce 217
avocado mayonnaise 218
barbecue sauce 218
Béchamel 216
blue cheese dip 218
bread sauce 216
butterscotch sauce 217
cheese sauce 216
chocolate sauce 212, 217
cocktail sauce 218
cold sauces and dips 85, 218
a 'fiery little number' (chilli) 217
Gorgonzola dip 99
green peppercorn cream 149
honey and mustard 32
horseradish cream 100, 182
horseradish sauce 21, 50, 73, 76
hot sauces 216–17
mustard sauce 128
onion gravy 217
oriental dipping sauce 153, 218
pepper sauce 217
salsa verde 218
sauce gribiche 218
tomato and horseradish sauce 218
tomato pasta (classic) sauce 216
tomato relish 26
for twice-cooked parsnips 169
white butter sauce 216
see also marinades
sausages
in breakfast omelette 24
pork sausage hot dog 32
in 'thrifty lentil supper' 104
scallops, in salad 92
scampi provençale 151
shallots
with parsnips and carrots 169
with rabbit legs 128
in salad 92
smoked mackerel
peppered, with beetroot and horseradish 73
in smoked fish paté 76
smoked salmon
bagels 34
baked potato filling 50
posh eggs 21
in smoked fish paté 76
see also salmon
smoothies 42–3
sole, cheesy sole with creamy spinach 143
soups, broths, stews and casseroles
Mediterranean chicken casserole 130

pea and spinach soup with horseradish cream 100
rabbit legs with roast shallots and mustard sauce 128
thrifty lentil supper 104
the ultimate pot noodle 62
white beans stew 133
winter warmer (potato soup) 98
spinach
creamy spinach with cheesy sole 143
with fettucine/tagliatelle 97
pea and spinach soup 100
with poached egg 22
spicy creamed 162
spring greens, in bubble and squeak 170
spring onions
in bubble and squeak 170
with pork chops (Chinese style) 106
squid
Asian squid salad 78
with penne and chorizo 55
stews see soups, broths, stews and casseroles
store cupboard items 240
strawberries, strawberry, lemon and mint smoothie 43
sushi 74

tartiflette 48
teriyaki-style salmon, pak choi and Chinese fried egg 154
thyme-roasted onions and potatoes 170
tomato and horseradish sauce 218
tomatoes
with bacon, roast field mushrooms anchovy 51
curried, with salmon and creamy peas 150
herby, on toast 37
with marinated lamb 118
meatballs with tomato and penne 60
in Moroccan salad 89
plum tomatoes with pasta and spinach 97
relish 26
in roast halibut with mozzarella 142
roast, with leg of lamb steaks 117
in spiced chicken rolls 68
tomato bread, chargrilled 33
tomato pasta (classic) sauce 216
warm smoked duck with cherry tomato and rocket bruschetta 69
as ingredient 18, 24, 28, 130
tortilla wrap with Morroccan lamb 59
trifle in a glass 191
truffle dressing 219

vegetables 160–85
emerald vegetables and miso chicken 136
spring vegetable salad and feta 90
Vietnamese crunchy salad 84
Vietnamese crunchy vegetable salad 84

walnut and mint dressing 219
watercress, with roast cod 149

yoghurt
with butter chicken 134
with fruity breakfast compôte 41
Middle Eastern spiced dip 85